W9-BTS-444

# Chinese Horoscopes

# Chinese Horoscopes

An easy guide to the Chinese
system of astrology

*Debbie Burns*

LANSDOWNE

Contents

# Introduction

## Why Chinese Astrology?

This book uncovers for you the secrets and essential aspects of Chinese astrology, in an easy-to-read format. You are presented with specific guidelines and techniques that will help you discover the following:

★ your own unique character and communication style
★ the unique characters and communication styles of others
★ ideal career paths for each sign
★ specific life challenges confronting each sign
★ compatibility ratings between the signs
★ how to blend Chinese astrology with the Chinese system of feng shui
★ how to blend Chinese astrology with the Western zodiac system, to achieve a greater degree of character awareness and more likelihood of compatibility with friends, lovers and business associates.

The information in this book will help you to gain a deeper understanding of who you are and how you relate to the world. You will acquire a richer appreciation of your own and others' individual uniqueness, and how the differences complement and support each other.

## How to Use this Book

This book has been written as a resource tool for Westerners who have little knowledge of or experience with Chinese beliefs, culture and practices relating to astrology and its place in our lives. It is presented in several stages:

We start with an overview of the origins and age-old beliefs of Chinese astrology, and how it was used then and is still used today to determine the likely success and/or challenges each individual will face in any life experience such as career, relationships, marriage, travel and health.

The essential aspects of the 12 animals of the Chinese horoscope, yin/yang energy and earthly elements are introduced. These three components are also linked, to help you appreciate their importance and their specific application to an individual's character.

Easy-to-read charts are provided so that you can determine your dominant, intimate (love) and ascendant signs and associated elements. All you need to know is the date and time of your birth.

You are then encouraged to study the detailed character profile for your dominant sign, and your compatibility with each of the other 11 signs.

To tailor your character profile further, you can study the character profiles for your intimate (love) sign and ascendant sign, and blend the traits of all three where appropriate, to arrive at a unique Chinese character profile.

You are introduced to the way of blending Chinese astrology with the Western Zodiac, to arrive at quite a comprehensive and integrated character analysis. (You can also use the same process to determine the character profiles of others.)

Finally, you are introduced to the way in which Chinese astrology complements the ancient practice of Chinese feng shui. There are some useful tips and techniques for enhancing your personal well-being and harmony with your environment.

# The Ancient System of Chinese Astrology

## The Legend

Legend states that, when the great Buddha found enlightenment beside an old oak tree, he invited all the animals to his kingdom to celebrate. Only 12 animals arrived, and Buddha promptly rewarded them by celebrating every new year in honor of each.

Hence, on a 12-year rotation, each animal is celebrated and its character traits are said to influence the events and personalities of newborns during the year. This is the basis of the system of Chinese astrology.

### The Order of the Animals

The order in which the animals arrived at Buddha's side is significant for understanding some of their characters. The legend tells of a great river that all the animals had to cross just before reaching Buddha. The first to arrive at the river were the Rat and the Ox. The Rat immediately saw that he needed the Ox's assistance to cross the raging river, and asked the Ox for a lift on his back. The Ox agreed. On reaching the other side, the smart-thinking Rat sprang from the Ox's back and raced up the riverbank, to be the first to arrive and, therefore, the first animal to be honored by Buddha. The hardworking Ox came in second.

The order of the 12 animals as they arrived at Buddha's side:

| ORDER | ANIMAL | MOTTO |
|-------|--------|-------|
| 1 | Rat | "I think" |
| 2 | Ox | "I am patient" |
| 3 | Tiger | "I have courage" |
| 4 | Hare | "I am discreet" |
| 5 | Dragon | "I am majestic" |
| 6 | Snake | "I have sense" |
| 7 | Horse | "I run free" |
| 8 | Sheep | "I adapt" |
| 9 | Monkey | "I entertain" |
| 10 | Rooster | "I am resilient" |
| 11 | Dog | "I am loyal" |
| 12 | Pig | "I am eager" |

## Origins of Chinese Astrology

The origins of Chinese astrology date back many thousands of years, and are steeped in ancient Chinese culture and philosophy. To understand Chinese astrology is to understand the essence of Chinese beliefs. Chinese philosophy proposes that everyone and everything has a specific place and purpose on Earth. The highest purpose is to achieve fulfillment and harmony within ourselves and with our environment. This is achieved through the careful balancing and maintenance of cycles, which integrate the concepts of life energy (yin/yang), and the earthly elements (wood, fire, earth, metal and water).

## Yin/Yang Energy

The Chinese believe all matter on earth, including all living things and even empty space, is comprised of "qi" energy. This energy takes one of two forms, either yang energy, which is positive/masculine, or yin energy, which is negative/feminine.

Yang energy is vibrant, noisy and fast, while yin is the polar opposite: subdued, quiet and slow. However, although they are exact opposites, each is dependent on the other for its existence. Some examples of both energies working in harmony:

YANG
Day
Summer
Sun
Sunrise
Life
Land

YIN
Night
Winter
Moon
Sunset
Death
Sea

*The concept of yin/yang energy plays*
*a central role in determining some common traits of,*
*and potential for compatibility between, the 12 animal signs.*

## The Earthly Elements

Life is said to be created, lived and destroyed through the dynamic interaction of the five earthly elements — wood, fire, earth, metal and water.

### Element cycles can be either productive or destructive.

The productive cycle: Wood produces fire, which produces earth, which produces metal, which produces water, which in turn produces wood.

The destructive cycle: wood destroys earth, which destroys water, which destroys fire, which destroys metal, which in turn destroys wood.

*Each animal sign has a natural element that influences its core traits. In addition, each animal is also influenced by the element governing its particular year, and this provides five distinct personality types within each animal group.*

## The Chinese Life Cycle

Following the Ganzhi Lunar Calendar, the Chinese record time in sixty-year cycles, which bring together each of the five earthly elements with each of the 12 animal years. This ensures that each element governs and influences each animal sign only once during a life cycle.

## Time Measurement in the East and the West

In the West, time is measured in solar years, i.e. the time it takes the Earth to orbit the sun, which is approximately 365 days. The Western new year occurs on the same day each year: January 1.

In contrast, the Chinese measure time in lunar years, i.e. the time it takes for the moon to orbit the Earth in a 12-year cycle. As the number of days per year can vary, each Chinese new year will occur on a slightly different date in either January or February. If you were born in January or February, check the Chinese Year Chart on page 12 for the specific date on which the Chinese new year began in that year. This will help you to identify your dominant animal sign correctly.

## How to Use Chinese Astrology

Chinese astrology provides new insights into our personal characters and relationships with others. It is a method that accesses ancient Chinese wisdom and culture used for centuries to determine the likely success and challenges in any of life's experiences — marriage, travel, having children, career, health.

### Year of Birth

*The year you were born determines your dominant sign.*

First, using the Chinese Year Chart on pages 12–15, look for your complementing animal and its earthly element for the year you were born. The traits of the animal sign and associated element will provide a detailed description of your *dominant* character, the "outer" you that is seen by others. Normally this is sufficient to obtain a basic understanding of your personality and that of others.

### Month of Birth

*The month you were born determines your love sign.*

The traits of the animal ruling the month you were born provide a more detailed analysis of your personality in intimate relationships. Use the Chinese Month and Daily Time Chart (page 15) to find the animal that rules your month. Then read the character description of this animal, particularly the description of the animal as a lover.

### Time of Birth

*The time you were born determines your ascendant sign.*

The animal sign ruling over the time of your birth is your *ascendant*, and is said to have a moderating effect on the traits of your dominant sign. The traits of this sign also describe your secret self — how you see and relate to yourself — which you normally keep hidden from others. The Chinese Month and Daily Time Chart on page 15 will reveal the animal that rules your time of birth.

Once you have identified the three major signs, read the detailed character descriptions that follow, noting what part of your character they govern.

EXAMPLE: DOB: 25/7/62    TIME: 9.50AM

| | | |
|---|---|---|
| **Dominant Sign** | *Tiger/Water:* | *Mainly displays these traits when with others* |
| **Love Sign** | *Sheep:* | *Displays these traits in intimate relationships* |
| **Ascendant Sign** | *Snake:* | *Moderates the dominant sign/the secret or hidden you.* |

***Pure signs occur when dominant and ascendant signs are the same.***

| Year | Dates | Animal | Element |
|------|-------|--------|---------|
| 1912 | Feb. 2 | Rat | Water |
| 1913 | Feb. 6 | Ox | Water |
| 1914 | Jan. 26 | Tiger | Wood |
| 1915 | Feb. 14 | Hare | Wood |
| 1916 | Feb. 3 | Dragon | Fire |
| 1917 | Jan. 23 | Snake | Fire |
| 1918 | Feb. 11 | Horse | Earth |
| 1919 | Feb. 1 | Sheep | Earth |
| 1920 | Feb. 20 | Monkey | Metal |
| 1921 | Feb. 8 | Rooster | Metal |
| 1922 | Jan. 28 | Dog | Water |
| 1923 | Feb. 16 | Pig | Water |
| 1924* | Feb. 5 | Rat | Wood |
| 1925 | Jan. 25 | Ox | Wood |
| 1926 | Feb. 13 | Tiger | Fire |
| 1927 | Feb. 2 | Hare | Fire |
| 1928 | Jan. 23 | Dragon | Earth |
| 1929 | Feb. 10 | Snake | Earth |
| 1930 | Jan. 30 | Horse | Metal |
| 1931 | Feb. 17 | Sheep | Metal |
| 1932 | Feb. 6 | Monkey | Water |
| 1933 | Jan. 26 | Rooster | Water |
| 1934 | Feb. 14 | Dog | Wood |
| 1935 | Feb. 4 | Pig | Wood |
| 1936 | Jan. 24 | Rat | Fire |
| 1937 | Feb. 11 | Ox | Fire |
| 1938 | Jan. 31 | Tiger | Earth |
| 1939 | Feb. 19 | Hare | Earth |
| 1940 | Feb. 8 | Dragon | Metal |
| 1941 | Jan. 27 | Snake | Metal |

| YEAR | DATES | ANIMAL | ELEMENT |
|------|-------|--------|---------|
| 1942 | Feb. 15 | Horse | Water |
| 1943 | Feb. 5 | Sheep | Water |
| 1944 | Jan. 25 | Monkey | Wood |
| 1945 | Feb. 13 | Rooster | Wood |
| 1946 | Feb. 2 | Dog | Fire |
| 1947 | Jan. 21 | Pig | Fire |
| 1948 | Feb. 10 | Rat | Earth |
| 1949 | Jan. 29 | Ox | Earth |
| 1950 | Feb. 17 | Tiger | Metal |
| 1951 | Feb. 6 | Hare | Metal |
| 1952 | Jan. 27 | Dragon | Water |
| 1953 | Feb. 14 | Snake | Water |
| 1954 | Feb. 3 | Horse | Wood |
| 1955 | Jan. 24 | Sheep | Wood |
| 1956 | Feb. 12 | Monkey | Fire |
| 1957 | Jan. 31 | Rooster | Fire |
| 1958 | Feb. 18 | Dog | Earth |
| 1959 | Feb. 8 | Pig | Earth |
| 1960 | Jan. 28 | Rat | Metal |
| 1961 | Feb. 15 | Ox | Metal |
| 1962 | Feb. 5 | Tiger | Water |
| 1963 | Jan. 25 | Hare | Water |
| 1964 | Feb. 13 | Dragon | Wood |
| 1965 | Feb. 2 | Snake | Wood |
| 1966 | Jan. 21 | Horse | Fire |
| 1967 | Feb. 9 | Sheep | Fire |
| 1968 | Jan. 30 | Monkey | Earth |
| 1969 | Feb. 17 | Rooster | Earth |
| 1970 | Feb. 6 | Dog | Metal |
| 1971 | Jan. 27 | Pig | Metal |

| Year | Dates | Animal | Element |
|------|-------|--------|---------|
| 1972 | Jan. 16 | Rat | Water |
| 1973 | Feb. 3 | Ox | Water |
| 1974 | Jan. 23 | Tiger | Wood |
| 1975 | Feb. 11 | Hare | Wood |
| 1976 | Jan. 31 | Dragon | Fire |
| 1977 | Feb. 18 | Snake | Fire |
| 1978 | Feb. 7 | Horse | Earth |
| 1979 | Jan. 28 | Sheep | Earth |
| 1980 | Feb. 16 | Monkey | Metal |
| 1981 | Feb. 5 | Rooster | Metal |
| 1982 | Jan. 25 | Dog | Water |
| 1983 | Feb. 13 | Pig | Water |
| 1984* | Feb. 2 | Rat | Wood |
| 1985 | Feb. 20 | Ox | Wood |
| 1986 | Feb. 9 | Tiger | Fire |
| 1987 | Jan. 30 | Hare | Fire |
| 1988 | Feb. 17 | Dragon | Earth |
| 1989 | Feb. 6 | Snake | Earth |
| 1990 | Jan. 27 | Horse | Metal |
| 1991 | Feb. 15 | Sheep | Metal |
| 1992 | Feb. 4 | Monkey | Water |
| 1993 | Jan. 23 | Rooster | Water |
| 1994 | Feb. 10 | Dog | Wood |
| 1995 | Jan. 31 | Pig | Wood |
| 1996 | Feb. 19 | Rat | Fire |
| 1997 | Feb. 8 | Ox | Fire |
| 1998 | Jan. 28 | Tiger | Earth |
| 1999 | Feb. 16 | Hare | Earth |
| 2000 | Feb. 5 | Dragon | Metal |

| Year | Dates | Animal | Element |
|------|-------|--------|---------|
| 2001 | Jan. 24 | Snake | Metal |
| 2002 | Feb. 12 | Horse | Water |
| 2003 | Feb. 1 | Sheep | Water |
| 2004 | Jan. 22 | Monkey | Wood |
| 2005 | Feb. 9 | Rooster | Wood |
| 2006 | Jan. 29 | Dog | Fire |
| 2007 | Feb. 18 | Pig | Fire |
| 2008 | Feb. 7 | Rat | Earth |
| 2009 | Jan. 26 | Ox | Earth |
| 2010 | Feb. 14 | Tiger | Metal |
| 2011 | Feb. 3 | Hare | Metal |
| 2012 | Jan. 23 | Dragon | Water |
| 2013 | Feb. 10 | Snake | Water |
| 2014 | Jan. 31 | Horse | Wood |
| 2015 | Feb. 19 | Sheep | Wood |
| 2016 | Feb. 8 | Monkey | Fire |
| 2017 | Jan. 28 | Rooster | Fire |
| 2018 | Feb. 16 | Dog | Earth |
| 2019 | Feb. 5 | Pig | Earth |

*\* — the beginning of a new 60-year life cycle. The year 1984 starts the 78th Chinese life cycle.*

## Chinese Month and Daily Time Chart

| Rat | December | 11pm–1am |
| Ox | January | 1am–3am |
| Tiger | February | 3am–5am |
| Hare | March | 5am–7am |
| Dragon | April | 7am–9am |
| Snake | May | 9am–11am |
| Horse | June | 11am–1pm |
| Sheep | July | 1pm–3pm |
| Monkey | August | 3pm–5pm |
| Rooster | September | 5pm–7pm |
| Dog | October | 7pm–9pm |
| Pig | November | 9pm–11pm |

# Relationship Charts for Harmony in Love, Friendship and Professional Life

Each animal is said to have two main friends from each of the other 11 animal types who are ideal for all personal and business relationships and one enemy who is best avoided. All other animals have potential for compatibility and require various levels of effort for success.

## Ratings

5   Excellent:      a natural pairing, guaranteed to result in harmony and success.
4   Optimistic:     a beneficial and mostly positive relationship for both parties.
3   Good:           little conflict if time and effort are invested by both parties.
2   Challenging:    considerable work and understanding required.
1   Antagonistic:   best avoided, as both parties oppose each other on all fronts.

## Chart

See the following pages for relationship charts specific to each animal sign:
Rat: page 20 • Ox: page 24 • Tiger: page 28 • Hare: page 32 • Dragon: page 36 • Snake: page 40 • Horse: page 44 • Sheep: page 48 • Monkey: page 52 • Rooster: page 56 • Dog: page 60 • Pig: page 64

|         | Rat | Ox | Tiger | Hare | Dragon | Snake | Horse | Sheep | Monkey | Rooster | Dog | Pig |
|---------|-----|----|-------|------|--------|-------|-------|-------|--------|---------|-----|-----|
| Rat     | 3   | 4  | 2     | 4    | 5      | 4     | 1     | 2     | 5      | 2       | 3   | 3   |
| Ox      | 4   | 3  | 2     | 4    | 2      | 5     | 2     | 1     | 3      | 5       | 4   | 3   |
| Tiger   | 2   | 2  | 3     | 4    | 4      | 2     | 5     | 3     | 1      | 3       | 5   | 4   |
| Hare    | 4   | 4  | 4     | 3    | 2      | 3     | 2     | 5     | 2      | 1       | 3   | 5   |
| Dragon  | 5   | 2  | 4     | 2    | 3      | 4     | 3     | 2     | 5      | 3       | 1   | 4   |
| Snake   | 4   | 5  | 2     | 3    | 4      | 3     | 2     | 3     | 4      | 5       | 2   | 1   |
| Horse   | 1   | 2  | 5     | 2    | 3      | 2     | 3     | 4     | 3      | 3       | 5   | 4   |
| Sheep   | 2   | 1  | 3     | 5    | 2      | 3     | 4     | 3     | 4      | 2       | 4   | 5   |
| Monkey  | 5   | 3  | 1     | 2    | 5      | 4     | 3     | 4     | 3      | 4       | 2   | 2   |
| Rooster | 2   | 5  | 3     | 1    | 3      | 5     | 3     | 2     | 4      | 3       | 2   | 4   |
| Dog     | 3   | 4  | 5     | 3    | 1      | 2     | 5     | 4     | 2      | 2       | 3   | 4   |
| Pig     | 3   | 3  | 4     | 5    | 4      | 1     | 4     | 5     | 2      | 4       | 4   | 3   |

# Groups of Best Friends

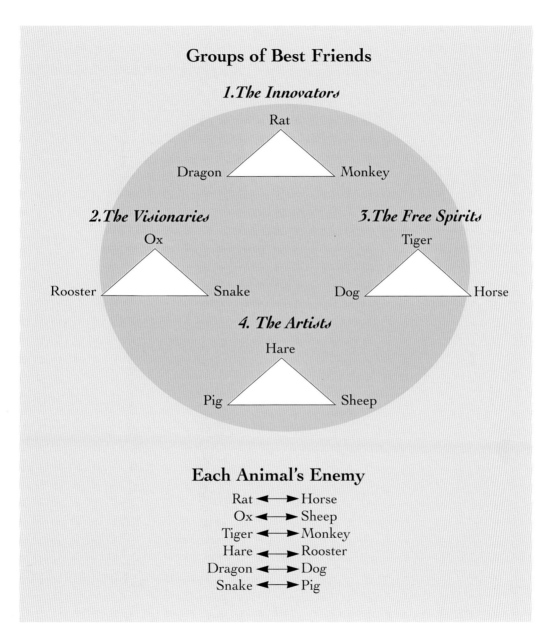

### 1.The Innovators

Rat

Dragon — Monkey

### 2.The Visionaries

Ox

Rooster — Snake

### 3.The Free Spirits

Tiger

Dog — Horse

### 4. The Artists

Hare

Pig — Sheep

## Each Animal's Enemy

Rat ⟷ Horse
Ox ⟷ Sheep
Tiger ⟷ Monkey
Hare ⟷ Rooster
Dragon ⟷ Dog
Snake ⟷ Pig

# The Rat

1912, 1924, 1936, 1948, 1960, 1972, 1984, 1996, 2008

**_Natural Energy: Yang_**
**_Natural Element: Water_**

Rats are chiefly concerned with power and material security. Ambition, success and wealth accumulation feature in their lives. Aided by their innate analytical and clear-thinking skills, they can devise elaborate plans that are assured of great success. Rats embody entrepreneurial and leadership skills.

Rats always appear smartly attired, witty and in control of their conduct. They make interesting and informed conversationalists who crave companionship and adore social gatherings. Rats have much public appeal and personal charm.

## Character Traits of Rats

Intelligent, industrious, resourceful, practical, self-motivated, thrifty, charming, communicative, compassionate, calm, observant, analytical, caring, discreet.

## Life Challenge for Rats

To overcome their inner fears and insecurities and diminish their nervous anxiety.

## The Rat Lover

Well equipped with quick wits, warm natures and stylish grooming, Rats have great success as attentive and debonair lovers. While young, they are drawn to the challenge of artful seduction using their extensive interpersonal skills. However, it is the quality of a committed, long-term relationship they desire most, and not a lifelong parade of superficial affairs.

Once committed they make gentle, loyal and protective partners who will always take time out to nurture their relationships and support and care for their partners. Rats' craving for their partners' approval and adoration will deter most from straying. Rats are not by nature promiscuous.

## The Rat Family Member

Rats make ideal providers for and protectors of their families. Rats take their family responsibilities seriously, and relish the roles of breadwinner and caretaker. As born leaders, they will want to be the more dominant partner, especially in decision making.

While practicality and thrift will be themes in their households, Rats are able to balance this with emotional warmth and sensitivity to those they love. Rats make considerate parents and fine role models, who will take an active part in their children's upbringing.

## The Rat Friend

Rats are also loyal to others they care about. Rats will prefer a few close and supportive friendships to numerous acquaintances, and are likely to keep childhood friendships for life.

Rats love to be esteemed, and will seek opportunities to give their friends advice. They make dependable, supportive and sincere friends, and love to entertain in small numbers, especially where food is involved. They often hold fabulous dinner parties.

## The Rat at Work

To remain stimulated, Rats need to be continually challenged intellectually in their work. Without adequate amounts of praise and recognition, Rats can become insecure and demotivated. This causes them to become restless and move from one job to the next.

As the "rat race" is their domain, they usually find the ride to the director's suite an easy trip, enjoying much success from their professional lives. To their colleagues Rats appear competent and emotionally self-contained, sometimes even a little secretive.

## Ideal Occupations for Rats

Business director, accountant, stockbroker, courtroom lawyer, auctioneer, politician.

## The Five Rat Types

### *Wood Rats: 1924, 1984*

The wood element heightens some core character traits in this Rat. Wood Rats are even more hardworking and anxious than other Rats. They hesitate when making decisions, preferring to gather lots of information and take much time in assessing situations before making a move.

### *Fire Rats: 1936, 1996*

Fire brings passion and burning enthusiasm to the Rat. Fire Rats are witty and charming, which adds to their already healthy dose of personal appeal. They are not above heroic deeds to impress a loved one, and can always attract an admiring crowd.

### *Earth Rats: 1948, 2008*

Earth provides this Rat with a good helping of practicality and wisdom. Earth Rats are the "old souls" of the Rat family. Their careful advice and wise counsel are their distinguishing features. Contrary to the usual traits of Rats, Earth Rats actually enjoy their own company.

### *Metal Rats: 1960*

Metal lends Rats a good dose of physical and mental strength. Metal Rats can have fixed ideas and can appear stubborn. Metal Rats are the most professionally successful of Rats, and usually do well as entrepreneurs.

### *Water Rats : 1912, 1972*

Water is the Rat's natural element, so the communication traits of the Rat is heightened. Water Rats are gifted communicators with an abundance of public appeal; they usually seek out public positions, and have the potential to be great orators or writers.

# Relationship Chart for Rats

*See page 16 for an explanation of the ratings used in this chart.*

| Rat & | Rating | Potential for Harmony in Love, Friendship and Professional Life |
|---|---|---|
| **Monkey** | 5 | Each will admire the other's quick wit and superior intelligence. Provided Rat remains tolerant of Monkey's antics, these two will initiate many schemes and ingenious plans together. |
| **Dragon** | 5 | Both are charged with energy and social charisma, and this will keep them satisfied. Each will be intuitive of the other's unspoken desires and will be able to meet the other's needs. |
| **Rat** | 3 | Good compatibility, particularly for business or friendships. Each will respect and understand the other. Unless the couple has a busy lifestyle, boredom will quickly set in. |
| **Ox** | 4 | A mutually rewarding partnership in any context. Rat's intelligence and ingenuity will complement Ox's physical tenacity. This pair could achieve much together. |
| **Tiger** | 2 | They have different perspectives on life, and clashing personal values and goals. Any attraction will be only fleeting, with Rat more interested in material accumulation and Tiger in adventure. |
| **Hare** | 4 | A mutually rewarding partnership in most contexts. Both animals are highly intuitive, and will be sympathetic toward each other and understanding of each other's needs. |
| **Snake** | 4 | Each will challenge the other's mental prowess, ensuring that a satisfying relationship evolves where each can learn much from the other. |
| **Sheep** | 2 | Interest in each other will be only fleeting and marginally rewarding. Rat will need more than just Sheep's adoring devotion to maintain interest, and Sheep will feel hurt by Rat's dwindling attraction. |
| **Rooster** | 2 | Each will be too quick to misjudge the other. Rat will view Rooster as too flamboyant and superficial, while Rooster will lose patience with Rat's cool and collected exterior. |
| **Dog** | 3 | This pairing can work if kept at friendship level. Both signs are nagged by personal insecurities, which will accumulate with the pairing. Dog will misinterpret Rat's secrecy as underhanded scheming. |
| **Pig** | 3 | The sensuous Pig will revel in Rat's material acquisitions. Rat will at first enjoy its provider role, and will then be likely to take Pig for granted; there is little hope for long-term success. |
| **Horse** | 1 | Both have healthy egos, which will be bruised regularly in this pairing. Horse will want physical and verbal freedom, which the politically correct Rat will be loath to respect. |

# The Ox

1913, 1925, 1937, 1949, 1961, 1973, 1985, 1997, 2009

***Natural Energy: Yin***
***Natural Element: Earth***

Oxen are the most physically powerful and sure-footed animals of the Chinese zodiac. No other sign can match them for physical endurance, tenacity and patience. Oxen are traditionalists at heart, who take life seriously, and will persevere through all manner of hardship to fulfill their goals and obligations.

Upfront, honest and practical, Oxen operate on clear values and beliefs and expect others to do the same. What you see is what you get with an Ox. They don't understand the notion of hidden agendas or double standards, and always practice what they preach.

For most of the time Oxen are placid, slow to anger and quick to forgive. However, those who cheat, lie or steal from them should beware. Once an Ox sees red, revenge can be explosive, severe — and unforgettable.

## Character Traits of the Ox

Reliable, patient, purposeful, conscientious, kind, determined, persevering, hardworking, sensuous, painstaking, dependable, stable, skillful, dexterous, confident, authoritative.

## Life Challenge for Oxen

To feel more comfortable with their feelings and more emotionally expressive.

## The Ox Lover

Work comes first and romance a distant second for this Ox. Hence Oxen are not likely to win or break many hearts during their lifetime, nor do they want to. Monogamy is the only game they want to play. Capable of deep and sensuous love, Oxen will settle down quickly into one lifelong, faithful relationship.

Oxen are renowned for their stamina and have an intense sensuous side to their nature. True moralists at heart, Oxen restrict their lovemaking to acceptable practices, and deplore kinky or perverse sexual acts. Having an Ox lover means being guaranteed a dependable, protective and kind partner.

## The Ox Family Member

Oxen make very reliable, stable and responsible children, siblings and parents. They love their homes, and believe in the value of family as the nucleus of modern society. They set high expectations for themselves and others, which can transform them into stern disciplinarians if their values are not shared.

Oxen make formidable protectors and dependable providers who will work day and night to ensure the needs of their family are met. It is through their actions — i.e. hard work — that Oxen express how much they feel for others.

## The Ox Friend

Kindly Oxen are capable of making everyone around them feel comfortable and secure. They love to entertain, particularly where fine food and wine are on offer. They are happy to indulge as a just reward for all their hard work.

Oxen prefer small gatherings to large, and intimate conversations to a lot of chatter. Confident in their social skills, Oxen love to recite entertaining sagas of triumphs over hardship and evil. It's marvelous being around an Ox friend who is in a jovial and indulgent mood.

## The Ox at Work

Extremely competent and capable individuals, Oxen shine in the work arena and can remain calm under pressure. As employees, Oxen are respected for their trustworthiness and dependability, and the way they ensure that even the most difficult projects are completed on time. As colleagues, Oxen are generous with their time and assistance (just remember the Chinese legend of how the Ox aided the Rat across the river on page 8).

As employers Oxen are open, honest and demanding. Most of an Ox's employees would claim their greatest work challenges, and hence successes, came with a clearly directed Ox as their superior. Oxen don't require accolades and promotions to maintain their enthusiasm. Their own personal sense of achievement is sufficient to motivate them — along with the occasional pay rise.

## Ideal Occupations for Oxen

Judge, police officer, statistician, administrator, ambulance driver, government worker.

## The Five Ox Types

### *Wood Oxen: 1925, 1985*

Wood brings even more stability to the Ox's calm character. Wood Oxen are extremely dependable, and live life by a very clear and specific code of ethics. They set and reach high goals in all areas of their lives and usually attain material wealth.

### *Fire Oxen: 1937, 1997*

The fire element can bring both dangerous volatility and vibrant enthusiasm to this Ox's character. Fire Oxen are more readily able and willing to express their emotions, especially their anger. Inflamed with passionate creativity, Fire Oxen are a powerhouse of achievement and will require a constant stream of new projects to keep them happy.

### *Earth Oxen: 1949, 2009*

The double earth element ensures these Oxen plenty of resourcefulness and wisdom. They are your typical Oxen, who display all of the Ox's core traits. Reliable and steadfast, Earth Oxen know what they want out of life and set out early with quiet patience and hard work to achieve their goals.

### *Metal Oxen: 1961*

Metal has the effect of strengthening the Ox's core character traits. Blessed with vision and logic, Metal Oxen make extremely capable business leaders. Metal Oxen are the most ambitious and materialistic of all Oxen, and will pursue their goals with tenacity.

### *Water Oxen: 1913, 1973*

Water brings eloquence, intuition and reflection to the Ox's character, traits it usually lacks. Water Oxen will be more focused on others throughout their lives, displaying competence as counselors or social workers. Wise, caring and logical, Water Oxen are the most altruistic of the group.

# Relationship Chart for Oxen

*See page 16 for an explanation of the ratings used in this chart.*

| Ox & | Rating | Potential for Harmony in Love, Friendship and Professional Life |
|------|--------|----------------------------------------------------------------|
| Rooster | 5 | Much success could come from this pairing, as flamboyant Rooster will attend to the social aspects of the relationship while Ox will attend to the detailed and physical work. |
| Snake | 5 | Much happiness could result from this pairing. Ox will provide Snake with stability and physical resources so they can meet common goals. Snake will entice Ox into lighter moods when necessary. |
| Rat | 4 | A mutually rewarding partnership in any context. Rat's intelligence and ingenuity will complement Ox's physical tenacity. This pair could achieve much together. |
| Ox | 3 | For the most part this pairing could work, as neither will ask too much from the other. However, life could become extremely dull, as all Oxen are quite serious types. |
| Tiger | 2 | In the wild, these two would be natural enemies. Both are physically powerful, and would want to dominate the relationship. This would lead to conflict and exhaustion on both parts. |
| Hare | 4 | Hare will be happy for Ox to dominate and provide. Hare's gentle optimism will act as a soothing balm to Ox's grueling pessimism. |
| Dragon | 2 | A powerful but thwarted combination. Ox won't be able to stand Dragon's passion for the unconventional. Dragon will quickly become bored and frustrated with Ox's fixation on routine. |
| Horse | 2 | A mutual lack of understanding and respect will unfold quickly with this pairing. Horse will crave freedom and excitement, and will soon leave the traditional and authoritative Ox. |
| Monkey | 3 | Ox will be fascinated by Monkey's sparkling wit, and Monkey will appreciate the attention. However, the attraction will be brief; Monkey craves change and Ox respects routine. |
| Dog | 4 | Both have common values such as loyalty and respect. This pairing could work, if Ox could lighten up and if Dog could maintain an understanding of Ox's temperament. |
| Pig | 3 | Both crave a peaceful and quiet home life. However, Pig may be irresponsible with money, which will frustrate Ox. Unless Pig can learn restraint, Ox will soon leave. |
| Sheep | 1 | Ox will have no respect for the excitable and morally deviant sheep, who will find no excitement in the dull Ox. This pairing is best avoided, as the values and beliefs of the two parties will be directly opposed. |

# The Tiger

1914, 1926, 1938, 1950, 1962, 1974, 1986, 1998, 2010

*Natural Energy: Yang*
*Natural Element: Wood*

Tiger's position as the third animal at Buddha's side denotes nobility and honor. In China, the Tiger, not the Lion, is believed to be king of all beasts. Those born under this noble sign display many leadership qualities and have a dynamic presence.

Tigers are born optimists who make daring plans and apply endless energy and purpose in carrying them out. They like to lead exciting and adventurous lives, full of thrills and spills, and they are attracted to danger like a moth to flame.

Blessed with luck and good fortune, most Tigers can conquer all manner of illness and despair to arrive triumphant, if a little weary, at old age. Only in retirement do they start to settle down and find some peace and contentment.

## Character Traits of Tigers

Charismatic, bold, protective, generous, curious, lucky, courageous, optimistic, idealistic, determined, intelligent, sensitive, benevolent, ambitious, loyal, honorable, reckless.

## Life Challenge for Tigers

To appreciate patience and heed the wise counsel of others.

## The Tiger Lover

Tigers are passionate to the extreme with unquenchable sexual thirsts. They are born flirts, who win their beloved's heart by performing heroic deeds and chasing them by arranging exciting and fun dates.

Tigers' attraction to change and adventure leaves them with little time to settle down and marry. They like to experiment with short bursts of monogamy, but the monotony and routine soon stifles them, ensuring rather a promiscuous lifestyle in the long run.

## The Tiger Family Member

Adorable, energetic and engaging as children, Tigers grow up to be the family's champion. Generous with their time, money and possessions, they will not hesitate to give everything up to ensure the safety of even the most distant relative — and they never think to ask for anything back.

Children are attracted to the fun-loving Tigers, who are naturally good parents, quite protective and encouraging. Provided they are given their freedom and space to roam, most Tigers are capable of successfully establishing a family in middle or later life.

## The Tiger Friend

Full of personality, humor and unmatched optimism, Tigers make entertaining and uplifting friends. They love having a busy social life, and can't resist the allure of parties. Gifted storytellers, they are a must at any social gathering, and they love to dress up.

Tigers also make loyal and dependable friends who will stand by their mates during all their ups and downs. As they can't stand lingering in misery for long themselves, they won't tolerate dark moods in others, and will go to all lengths to brighten up everyone's day.

## The Tiger at Work

Tigers make motivating managers and formidable leaders who quickly rise to positions of power. Their supremacy will be unmatched if they learn early to heed the counsel of those wiser and more reflective than themselves.

Tigers are loyal to their employers and supportive of their colleagues. Their honesty and desire to protect the less fortunate will often see them take up many causes; they deplore workplace injustice. Ambitious and talented, Tigers are attracted to the recognition and rewards a job can provide them.

## Ideal Occupations for Tigers

Entrepreneur, actor, writer, union leader, explorer, teacher, military leader.

## The Five Tiger Types

### *Wood Tigers: 1914, 1974*

The influence of double wood creates a very charming and socially oriented Tiger. Wood Tigers love to entertain, and be entertained in return. They are the life of the party, preferring to keep to a carefree existence, devoid of any commitments.

### *Fire Tigers: 1926, 1986*

Fire adds even more passion and energy to this Tiger's personality. Fire Tigers know only two speeds: flat out or full stop. They are constantly chasing new opportunities and frequently changing careers. Their hectic and stressful lifestyles can cause early burnout.

### *Earth Tigers: 1938, 1998*

The influence of the earth element provides the daring Tiger with much-needed stability and practicality. Earth Tigers are the most patient of all Tigers and the most likely to succeed in balancing their lives and achieving their long-range goals. Earth Tigers have a keen nurturing side to their characters, making them indulgent parents and partners.

### *Metal Tigers: 1950, 2010*

Loaded with added strength and vitality, Metal Tigers are the most ruthless and ambitious of all Tigers, rarely showing any sentimentality. They make commanding but inflexible figures in business, and often have fierce tempers.

### *Water Tigers: 1962*

Water Tigers are the most intuitive and calm of all Tigers, which ensures them a less volatile life. They operate from highly tuned instincts, and their gut feelings about people and things are usually correct. They make fair and just leaders, and are champions of life's "underdogs".

# Relationship Chart for Tigers

*See page 16 for an explanation of the ratings used in this chart.*

| *Tiger &* | *Rating* | *Potential for Harmony in Love, Friendship and Professional Life* |
|---|---|---|
| **Horse** | 5 | A beneficial pairing, where both could provide the other with the freedom and fanfare craved. Horse will encourage Tiger to pursue his or her dreams, and Tiger will reward Horse with lots of excitement. |
| **Dog** | 5 | There will be much understanding and respect between these two. Practical Dog will ease Tiger's impulsiveness, and energetic Tiger will chase away Dog's anxieties and inner doubts. |
| **Rat** | 2 | They have different perspectives on life, and their personal values and goals will clash. Any attraction will be only fleeting, with Rat more interested in material accumulation, and Tiger all for adventure. |
| **Ox** | 2 | In the wild these two are natural enemies. Both are physically powerful, and will want to dominate the relationship. This would lead to conflict, and exhaustion on both parts. |
| **Tiger** | 3 | A natural attraction, fueled by extra daring and thirst for adventure. With little patience or practicality between the two, a match of two Tigers would be too reckless and, in fact, extremely dangerous. |
| **Hare** | 4 | Flexible Hare will be happy for Tiger to take the lead. Tiger will feel appreciated and supported, and Hare will feel encouraged to take bigger risks. |
| **Dragon** | 4 | The members of this pair have much in common, and could live and work comfortably together. There will be opportunity for dynamic enterprise if both learn to respect each other's time in the limelight. |
| **Snake** | 2 | A one-sided attraction. Tiger won't be able to resist the aloof and mesmerizing Snake. However, Snake won't be attracted to the tactless Tiger, and will soon slither off to other, more elusive characters. |
| **Sheep** | 3 | Apart from their high sex drives, Sheep and Tiger will have little in common. Sheep will be hurt by Tiger's need for adventure and personal space. Tiger will soon feel too claustrophobic in this pairing. |
| **Rooster** | 3 | Each will be attracted to each other's appearance, but they have very different communication styles. Rooster will henpeck Tiger on every detail, which will frustrate carefree Tiger no end. |
| **Pig** | 4 | Home-loving Pig will be happy and appreciative if Tiger acts as provider and protector. Tiger will bask in Pig's esteem and indulgent nature. |
| **Monkey** | 1 | Both are competitive and impatient daredevils, ensuring many calamities if they pair up. Tiger will be supersensitive to Monkey's pranks, and Monkey will soon get bored with Tiger's lack of appreciation. |

# The Hare

1915, 1927, 1939, 1951, 1963, 1975, 1987, 1999, 2011

*Natural Energy: Yin*
*Natural Element: Wood*

As the fourth animal to reach Buddha's side, the Hare holds the position of harmony and flexibility. Hares are generally kind and sensitive characters who detest open conflict, preferring to manage their disputes with skillful diplomacy, intelligence and tact.

Hares approach life with cautious detachment, preferring the role of reflective observer rather than active participant. They have a tendency to choose safe and conservative options and goals, which can mean fewer large-scale rewards, and less upheaval in their lives.

Hares are happy, discreet and refined people.

### Character Traits of Hares

Diplomatic, peaceful, sensitive, intuitive, reflective, refined, stylish, moderate, caring, quiet, friendly, alert, even-tempered, clever, sexy, intelligent.

### Life Challenge for Hares

To overcome a fear of change, and take more risks in life.

### The Hare Lover

The Hare is a fertile sign in China, and this means that clandestine romance and intimate delights are the key indulgences of the amorous Hare. The symbol of fertility probably originates from Hares' physical attunement with nature and the cycles of life, which makes them highly sensitive to their own reproductive cycles.

While they are generally passive lovers, Hares always practice discretion. They make lighthearted teasers who are attracted to older and wiser characters. Security and protection are important qualities that Hares expect their intimate relationships to provide.

## The Hare Family Member

Hares make easygoing partners who relish the roles of homemaker and parent. Blessed with refinement and good taste, Hares can be meticulous about the decor and maintenance of their homes. Comfort is also a key need, and this ensures that everyone can feel relaxed in the Hare's home.

Hares go to great lengths to ensure that harmonious relationships are maintained in the family, and will not abide any tantrums or fighting on the part of their children and partners. They have a calming influence and like to practice what they preach.

## The Hare Friend

Hares make caring and adaptable friends, whom others feel quite comfortable around at all times of the day and night. Hares find the company of a few close friends reassuring, and can prefer this to solitude. Hence they will invest a lot of time in cultivating friendships.

Their love of nature and curiosity about the world make them keen travelers and flexible traveling companions.

## The Hare at Work

Hares prefer to work on their own in an evenly paced and calm environment. Independent occupations that can employ their good taste and refinement or kinship with the environment will feed their souls. Hares' intuition and intelligence equip them well in the business world, especially as diplomats or mediators..

In the workplace, Hares' flexibility and genuine concern for others ensure they can fit easily into any team. Provided the workplace is not marked by constant change and open hostility, Hares can perform well in numerous positions and types of businesses.

## Ideal Occupations for Hares

Diplomat, antique dealer, interior decorator, art collector, biologist, sociologist, naturalist, forester, counselor, mediator.

## The Five Hare Types

### *Wood Hares: 1915, 1975*

The emphasis of double wood produces very generous, altruistic Hares who are preoccupied with receiving and sharing material wealth. Wood Hares are also quite creative and artistic, and will frequently choose the arts to express their talents; they will also commit to frequent travel for inspiration.

### *Fire Hares: 1927, 1987*

The presence of fire adds passion and more daring to the normally reticent Hare. Skilled with verbal dexterity, Fire Hares make great debaters, and politicians who are not too fearful of the public eye when pursuing justice for minority groups. With their additional energy, Fire Hares also demonstrate more dedication to long-range plans than other Hares.

### *Earth Hares: 1939, 1999*

The earth element adds to the Hare's already balanced nature, and this makes Earth Hares fairly pragmatic and moralistic. They are serious and hard-working characters who will follow tradition and apply caution when making decisions.

### *Metal Hares: 1951, 2011*

The metal element provides Hares with much-needed tenacity and courage. Metal Hares are the least emotional of all Hares, and are very adept in the political and business arena. They are also ambitious, and will find much success due to their visionary skills. Metal Hares need to watch that they do not become too rigid in their beliefs.

### *Water Hares: 1963*

The water element deepens Hares' already intuitive and sensitive nature, making Water Hares extremely sensitive to their surroundings and others' hardships. Plagued by irrational fears and insecurity, Water Hares may become rather withdrawn and extremely passive.

# Relationship Chart for Hares

*See page 16 for an explanation of the ratings used in this chart.*

| Hare & | Rating | Potential for Harmony in Love, Friendship and Professional Life |
|---|---|---|
| Pig | 5 | Both have peaceful and tolerant natures, and will be able to provide each other with gentle, loving care. Pig will provide strength and openness, and Hare will provide practicality. |
| Sheep | 5 | Both have loving and caring natures, and will draw out and motivate each other. Hare will help Sheep set priorities for his or her responsibilities. Sheep will give Hare unconditional love. |
| Rat | 4 | A mutually rewarding partnership in most contexts. Both animals are highly intuitive and will be sympathetic toward each other and understanding of each other's needs. |
| Ox | 4 | Hare will be happy for Ox to dominate and provide. Hare's gentle optimism will act as a soothing balm to Ox's grueling pessimism. |
| Tiger | 4 | Flexible Hare will be happy for Tiger to take the lead. Tiger will feel appreciated and supported, and Hare will be encouraged to take bigger risks. |
| Hare | 3 | A common understanding and calmness will ensure there are few disagreements between these two. However, this union will be extremely passive and is likely to buckle under outside pressure. |
| Dragon | 2 | The magnetic and impulsive Dragon will be too much for the reserved and cautious Hare. Dragon will quickly tire of Hare's lack of strength. |
| Snake | 3 | Their mutual tact and political correctness will keep these two respecting each other. Their secretive sides could lead to mutual suspicion if open communication is not maintained. |
| Horse | 2 | Much frustration and misunderstanding will mark this pairing. Energetic and fiery Horse will lose patience with the steady pace and passivity of Hare. |
| Monkey | 2 | Both are witty and inventive, which will ensure an attraction. However, Monkey will always be breaking social rules and norms, which Hare won't tolerate for long. |
| Dog | 3 | Hare and Dog have similar temperaments, and are likely to put each other's needs before their own. While there will be little conflict, there will also be not much challenge between them or much initiative taken. |
| Rooster | 1 | Rooster and Hare are poles apart in their values and social styles, and hence little respect can be achieved. Hare is considerate and understated, and Rooster is quite self-absorbed. |

# The Dragon

1916, 1928, 1940, 1952, 1964, 1976, 1988, 2000, 2012

*Natural Energy: Yang*
*Natural Element: Earth*

In China, Dragons are mythical animals who live in the heavens and command the forces of nature, such as rain, wind, storm and flood. They are viewed as awesome and volatile creatures who are fairly unpredictable. Their fifth position at Buddha's side denotes power and reverence.

Dragons are magnetic, intelligent and extremely self-confident, able to brush aside life's obstacles easily to ensure much personal success. They love to be the focus of attention and at the helm of every project. Their personal charisma holds others in awe and admiration. Dragons are free spirits, sensitive to their environment and in constant need of new experiences and adventures. They also have fiery tempers.

## Character Traits of Dragons

Dynamic, lucky, exciting, idealistic, enthusiastic, confident, vital, extravagant, energetic, physical, powerful, creative, ambitious, adventurous, brave, optimistic, intelligent.

## Life Challenge for Dragons

To appreciate commitment, inner calm and the feelings of others.

## The Dragon Lover

Dragons have a thirst for love, and will focus a lot of energy on their intimate relationships. As lovers they are passionate, intense and possessive. They are both physically and emotionally demanding of their partners.

Dragons love to be in love, and will be often. They are great in the heady early days of new romance, but dislike the routine and commitment necessary for long-term relationships. It is variety and the unusual that attract these feisty free spirits.

## The Dragon Family Member

Dragon children are good students and quite athletic, preferring to spend their time outdoors; they enjoy being at school if they are kept motivated. As parents, they will keep their families busy taking regular holidays and hosting many social events.

Domestic situations do not usually attract Dragons, as they suffer from claustrophobia and fear boredom. If they do finally settle down, Dragons build ultra-modern homes close to nature — for example, near oceans or on mountain tops — and they will frequently redecorate.

## The Dragon Friend

Dragons are extroverts who need lots of friends to keep them occupied and happy. They seek out exciting and interesting people who are likewise attracted to change, mystery and new adventures. Extremely fashion conscious, they are always stylish and maintain trendy wardrobes.

They can always be counted on to magnify the good times, but can be a little unreliable during the bad. It is also advisable to keep them in good spirits, as they have fiery tempers when angered.

## The Dragon at Work

Dragons are renowned visionaries who are talented strategists in business. They command leadership positions. Control and decision-making power are essential in any role they take on.

Dragons may sometimes question their own brilliance and obvious talents and abilities; their facade of extreme confidence may sometimes cover up personal insecurities.

## Ideal Occupations for Dragons

Visual artist, photo-journalist, adventurer, athlete, artist, business director, entrepreneur, military leader.

## The Five Dragon Types

### *Wood Dragons: 1964*

The presence of wood provides Dragons with much creative talent and innovation. Wood Dragons are also renowned for their beauty, elegance and refinement, and can often be found in dominant social positions. They may also be widely admired trendsetters.

### *Fire Dragons: 1916, 1976*

The fire element adds even more vibrancy and passion to the already quite dynamic Dragon. Fire Dragons have huge personalities and are obsessed with their social life. They are very exciting and entertaining people with generous hearts. Their only downfall is their explosive temper, which luckily flares only rarely.

### *Earth Dragons: 1928, 1988*

The presence of double earth ensures that these Dragons are more grounded and emotionally balanced than others. Earth Dragons are more able than other Dragons to work as part of a team and provide wise counsel. They are lucky to escape the emotional torrents experienced by other Dragons, which makes them quite comfortable with who and what they are.

### *Metal Dragons: 1940, 2000*

The metal element adds strength to many of the Dragon's qualities. Metal Dragons are exhibitionists and opinionated, and seek out positions where they will be noticed and heard. With their huge egos, Metal Dragons have a hard time dealing with reality and routine.

### *Water Dragons: 1952, 2012*

The water element has these Dragons focused on others' well-being rather than their own. Water Dragons are also more diplomatic and intuitive, and seek out positions that focus on correcting social problems. Water tends to have a calming effect, and this ensures that Water Dragons do not come across too strongly with others.

# Relationship Chart for Dragons

*See page 16 for an explanation of the ratings used in this chart.*

| Dragon & | Rating | Potential for Harmony in Love, Friendship and Professional Life |
|---|---|---|
| **Rat** | 5 | Both animals are charged with energy and social charisma, which will keep them satisfied. Each will be intuitive of the other's unspoken desires and will be able to meet the other's needs. |
| **Monkey** | 5 | Dragon will be attracted to Monkey's charm and wit, and Monkey to Dragon's personal power. Monkey will be happy for Dragon to dominate, and the two will live easily together. |
| **Ox** | 2 | A powerful combination, but one that will soon be thwarted. Ox won't be able to stand Dragon's passion for the unconventional. Dragon will quickly become bored and frustrated with Ox's fixation on routine. |
| **Tiger** | 4 | This pair will have much in common, and will be able to live and work comfortably together. There is opportunity for dynamic enterprise if each learns to respect the other's time in the limelight. |
| **Hare** | 2 | The magnetic and impulsive Dragon will be too much for the reserved and cautious Hare. Dragon will quickly tire of the Hare's lack of strength. |
| **Dragon** | 3 | A meeting of extremes, guaranteed to highlight the best and the worst in the two characters. This relationship will serve only as a personal reflection, and as an opportunity for introspection. |
| **Snake** | 4 | An extremely attractive match. Dragon will feel respected and socially elevated by Snake's beauty and social graces. Snake is smart enough to appreciate Dragon's dynamic appeal. |
| **Horse** | 3 | The energy and enthusiasm levels match in this pairing. Provided Dragon and Horse can agree on their goals and provide enough space for their larger-than-life personalities, a relationship will last. |
| **Sheep** | 2 | This pair are stark opposites and will find it hard to find anything in common or to appreciate anything in the other. Dragon will demand adventure, while Sheep will want stability. |
| **Rooster** | 3 | Mutual attraction will be assured as both Rooster and Dragon regularly attract the limelight, and share it. Unfortunately, neither one will be very interested in a committed relationship with the other. |
| **Pig** | 4 | This pairing is an example of opposites attracting. Dramatic Dragon will sweep easygoing Pig off his or her feet. Pig will reward Dragon with adoration and esteem. |
| **Dog** | 1 | There will be little attraction between these two. Their moral beliefs will vary in the extreme. Egotistical Dragon will have Dog snapping often, and exhausting fights will result. |

# The Snake

1917, 1929, 1941, 1953, 1965, 1977, 1989, 2001, 2013

*Natural Energy: Yin*
*Natural Element: Fire*

Snake's sixth position at Buddha's side denotes centrality and wisdom, a position of quiet but distinct influence. Snakes are able to draw strength and power effortlessly from those around them. Snake women are also believed to be the most beautiful and alluring of all the signs.

Snakes are true intellectuals, preferring the world of thought to the world of action. They demonstrate much self-control and appropriate emotional detachment. Snakes probably wrote the rules of political correctness! Cultured and sophisticated, Snakes are conservative yet tasteful, and are able to acquire material wealth easily.

## Character Traits of Snakes

Alert, intelligent, intuitive, wise, calculating, conservative, cautious, mysterious, alluring, elegant, shrewd, sophisticated, sensual, reflective, organized.

## Life Challenge for Snakes

To become more physically involved in their world, and more emotionally accessible.

## The Snake Lover

The alluring Snakes are gifted seducers, able to entrance everyone around them with their hypnotic gaze and sensual conversation. Once committed, Snakes are capable of deep and enduring love for their partners.

Snakes are smart in the love arena, choosing partners according to their perceived personal or social benefits. While they can often appear cold and aloof, this demonstration of emotional detachment is just part of their intricate plan of entrapment.

## The Snake Family Member

The stability and constancy of family and home provide Snakes with the structured and reliable environment they prefer. Snakes make good homemakers who are gifted with money-management skills and who will ensure their families do not want for anything.

Deeply attached to their partners and children, Snakes can be a little oversensitive, and protective toward their loved ones. These traits are also evident in Snake children, who are very sensitive to family quarrels. They are protective of their siblings, but don't like them gaining too much attention from their parents. This brings out their jealous streak.

## The Snake Friend

Snakes are very sociable and are addicted party-goers. They prefer controlled indoor activities and are fascinated by cultural pursuits. Hence, they will spend much of their social time arranging and attending trips to theaters, galleries and museums with their friends.

Snakes appreciate the finer things in life and will enjoy luxuriating in opulence. Fine dining and vintage wines are always popular with Snakes, who will hold many understated but exquisite dinner parties.

## The Snake at Work

Snakes often find success later in life, as they spend their younger years cultivating their social and artistic interests. Once they become career oriented, Snakes demonstrate keen business acumen and political savvy. They won't necessarily seek obvious positions of power, preferring roles where they can influence and counsel the figureheads on strategic directions.

Snakes are the best networkers of the zodiac. They have excellent organizational skills and are extremely efficient at everything they do.

Snakes appear to achieve much with very little effort. Generally liked in the workplace, they can sometimes be accused of having a hidden agenda when dealing with others.

## Ideal Occupations for Snakes

Scientist, academic, art or food critic, writer, poet, philosopher, human resource manager, interior designer.

## The Five Snake Types

### *Wood Snakes: 1965*

The presence of wood makes Snakes quite laid back and happy to indulge in their leisure and cultural pursuits, rather than focusing on their careers. Hence, Wood Snakes' occupations of choice will be ones that are sedate and independent — writing, for example. This will enable them to blend their work perfectly with their social and cultural activities.

### *Fire Snakes: 1917, 1977*

Fire Snakes are in their natural element, and this serves to accentuate their already impressive list of traits. Fire Snakes will have far more energy and dynamic presence than other Snakes and are likely to set many professionals goals, which they will achieve with little effort.

### *Earth Snakes: 1929, 1989*

Earth balances the Snake's sometimes fragile inner peace, and in the Earth Snake a more relaxed and openly communicative Snake emerges. Earth Snakes are calm and gentle people who are genuinely concerned about others. They are not as manipulative or secretive as other Snakes.

### *Metal Snakes: 1941, 2001*

Metal brings unwavering strength and seriousness to the Snake's character, ensuring Metal Snakes a very healthy ego. Metal Snakes are extremely confident of their own abilities and are perfectionists in everything they do. They are also ambitious and capable of working long and hard to achieve their goals.

### *Water Snakes: 1953, 2013*

Both water and Snakes are highly intuitive, and the combination means that Water Snakes will be revered for their accurate perceptions and feelings. Some Water Snakes are naturally gifted with clairvoyance, and will at the least make highly valued counselors and advisors to business and political leaders.

# Relationship Chart for Snakes

*See page 16 for an explanation of the ratings used in this chart.*

| Snake & | Rating | Potential for Harmony in Love, Friendship and Professional Life |
|---------|--------|---------------------------------------------------------------|
| Ox | 5 | Much happiness could come from this pairing. Ox will provide Snake with stability and physical resources for meeting their common goals. Snake will entice Ox into lighter moods when necessary. |
| Rooster | 5 | Each will complement and respect the other. Snake will admire Rooster's flamboyant social presence. Rooster will appreciate Snake's wise counsel and social refinement. |
| Rat | 4 | Each will challenge the other's mental abilities, ensuring that a satisfying relationship evolves where each can learn much from the other. |
| Tiger | 2 | A one-sided attraction. Tiger won't be able to resist the aloof and enchanting Snake. However, Snake will not be attracted to tactless Tiger and will soon slither off to other, more elusive characters. |
| Hare | 3 | Their common tact and political correctness will keep these two respecting each other. However, the secretive side to both of these animals may lead to suspicion if open communication is not maintained. |
| Dragon | 4 | An extremely attractive match. Dragon will feel respected and socially elevated by Snake's beauty and social graces. Snake will be smart enough to appreciate Dragon's dynamic appeal. |
| Snake | 3 | These two will have much hypnotic attraction to each other but, as Snake can be secretive and jealous, it is best for their emotional well-being that two Snakes do not stay long together. |
| Horse | 2 | A case of opposites attracting at first sight. Snake will be impressed with Horse's free spirit and Horse will be attracted to Snake's charm. They will soon find little else to appreciate. |
| Sheep | 3 | There will be enough mutual interest in art, music and theater for these two to be friends. However, Sheep is quite sentimental and sensitive, and will soon be put off by Snake's detachment. |
| Monkey | 4 | There is enough mental dexterity here to ensure success as business partners. Snake will provide the logic, and Monkey the calculated risks. |
| Dog | 2 | In the long run, this combination will work only with difficulty. Snake tends to be intense and secretive, and the honorable and upfront Dog is likely to see this as deceit. |
| Pig | 1 | Pig is open and generous with affection. Snake is secretive, and keeps his or her feelings to his or herself. Each just won't be able to understand or respect the other. |

# The Horse

1918, 1930, 1942, 1954, 1966, 1978, 1990, 2002, 2014

*Natural Energy: Yang*
*Natural Element: Fire*

Horse's seventh position at Buddha's side represents youthful vitality and freedom. People born in Horse years are by nature active, adventurous, restless and young at heart. Horse people have so much excess energy that they will continually involve themselves in daredevil outdoor and sporty pursuits in the vain hope of tiring themselves out. Horses are the Chinese zodiac's absolute free spirits. If their freedom is hindered in any way they may be prone to bouts of claustrophobia.

Horses' need for freedom extends into all areas of their lives. They are extroverts who adore company and all manner of social activities, where they prefer to be the focus of attention at social gatherings. Never afraid to speak their minds, Horses rush into conversations and debates, no matter how little they may know about the subject. They tend to take on causes, and their impatience and lack of caution can be challenges.

## Character Traits of Horses

Independent, headstrong, hardworking, talkative, energetic, dexterous, sociable, strong, bold, intelligent, confident, brave, opportunistic, ambitious, competitive, youthful.

## Life Challenge for Horses

To integrate quiet thought, reflection, focus and tenacity into their daily lives.

## The Horse Lover

Most Horses are physically attractive, and will remain so for much of their lives. Their charisma and energy act like a magnet. Horses are physically exhausting as lovers! Horses love a challenge, and will throw themselves into the game of love with abandon and zest. Dashing and daring, Horses excel as heroic lovers who come galloping in to rescue their fair damsels or handsome males from less attractive suitors. Unfortunately, their persistent restlessness and attraction to greener pastures will have them quickly moving on to other, unexplored terrain. Horse affairs are always short — but memorable.

## The Horse Family Member

It is rare for Horses to settle down, and the only way to achieve this is if their partners offer much adoration, praise and understanding. Horses detest jealousy, and their partners will need to learn quickly to give them plenty of room in the relationship.

Once settled, Horses make good protectors of their families and revel in their children's company. Horses are dexterous and are likely to build their family homes singlehandedly, along with much of the furniture. Provided they are kept challenged and interested professionally, they can make steady and generous providers.

## The Horse Friend

There's no such thing as a quiet, intimate get-together when a Horse is involved. Even during a quick catch-up over coffee, Horses will dominate the conversation, and they may also try to coax you into a brisk walk. Horses love company, but will set the pace in all shared activities.

Horse friends are cheery and optimistic, and will do their best to rouse others from their doldrums. On a whim they will suggest all manner of things to do, and will expect their pals to jump with enthusiasm. Horses make good protectors of their friends.

## The Horse at Work

Horses are best in front-line, people-oriented positions where they can use their extensive interpersonal skills to the full. They are advised to seek mobile, outdoor positions that will challenge them, keep them on the move and in a variety of environments.

Their manual skills can also earn them a good living, so building; cabinetmaking or craftwork may suit them. If restlessness persists, anything in the travel industry will keep them happily occupied.

## Ideal Occupations for Horses

Photographer, sales person, technician, builder, jockey, racing-car driver, tour operator.

## The Five Horse Types

### *Wood Horses: 1954, 2014*

Wood helps to balance the emotions of the volatile Horse, ensuring that Wood Horses appear more calm and relaxed with themselves and with others. Emotionally stable Wood Horses find it easier than other Horses to settle down and commit to long-term plans.

### *Fire Horses: 1966*

Double fire means these Horses are even more passionate and frantic daredevils than the other types. It is impossible to tame Fire Horses and have them commit to any plan or relationship. They are true free spirits, destined to travel the planet unhindered.

### *Earth Horses: 1918, 1978*

The earth element provides these Horses with much-needed stability and resourcefulness. Earth Horses are more serious and determined than others, and more likely to accomplish all they set out to achieve in life.

### *Metal Horses: 1930, 1990*

Metal provides Horses with more tenacity and resolution. Metal Horses are headstrong, with volatile emotions. To keep them happy, they need to be given a lot of freedom, motivation and praise in their relationships and their work.

### *Water Horses: 1942, 2002*

Water strengthens the Horse's communication skills and artistic ability. Water Horses make entertaining storytellers and imaginative artists who require more freedom of expression and speech than they do physical space.

# Relationship Chart for Horses

*See page 16 for an explanation of the ratings used in this chart.*

| Horse & | Rating | Potential for Harmony in Love, Friendship and Professional Life |
|---------|--------|----------------------------------------------------------------|
| **Tiger** | 5 | A beneficial pairing, where each will be able to provide the other with the freedom and fanfare craved. Horse will encourage Tiger to pursue his or her dreams, and Tiger will reward Horse with lots of excitement. |
| **Dog** | 5 | A solid relationship, based on similar temperaments and mutual respect. Dog will understand Horse's need for freedom, and will be supportive. Horse will openly demonstrate his or her appreciation, which Dog will cherish. |
| **Ox** | 2 | A mutual lack of understanding and respect will unfold quickly with this pairing. Horse will crave freedom and excitement, and will soon leave the traditional and authoritative Ox. |
| **Hare** | 2 | Much frustration and misunderstanding will mark this pairing. Energetic and fiery Horse will lose patience with the steady pace and passivity of Hare. |
| **Dragon** | 3 | The energy and enthusiasm levels will match in this pairing. Provided Dragon and Horse can agree on their goals, and provide enough space for the other's larger-than-life personality, the relationship will last. |
| **Snake** | 2 | A case of opposites attracting at first sight. Snake will be impressed with Horse's free spirit, and Horse will be attracted to Snake's charm. They will soon find little else to appreciate. |
| **Horse** | 3 | Provided neither asks for commitment from the other, these two spirited adventurers will end up traveling the world together. Both are reckless, which may lead to drama along the way. |
| **Sheep** | 4 | These two will have much in common, especially creative ability, which they will encourage and help to develop in the other. The only hurdle will be Horse's lack of commitment. |
| **Monkey** | 3 | Each will be attracted to the other's energy and enthusiasm. However, Horse wear his or her hearts on his or her sleeve, and can be a little gullible, which secretive Monkey will not appreciate. |
| **Rooster** | 3 | Both are lively and entertaining, which will ensure an initial attraction. However, Rooster will want to control the relationship, which will cause Horse to bolt. |
| **Pig** | 4 | This couple will be popular, and will have an active social life together. At some point Horse will want to travel abroad, and Pig will want to stay at home. |
| **Rat** | 1 | Both have healthy egos, which will be bruised regularly in this pairing. The Horse will want physical and verbal freedom, which politically correct Rat will be loath to respect. |

# The Sheep

1919, 1931, 1943, 1955, 1967, 1979, 1991, 2003, 2015

*Natural Energy: Yin*
*Natural Element: Earth*

Sheep's eighth position at Buddha's side is associated with peace and serenity. Sheep are introverts, and are quiet, patient and friendly. Extreme pacifists, they detest violence in any form. They live by their strong values and beliefs, and have a keen sense of right and wrong.

Sheep have imaginative and creative minds, and are often gifted artists, writers and musicians. Their calm and introspective personalities also make them good listeners, who like to hear all points of view before forming a judgment or making a decision.

## Character Traits of Sheep

Creative, imaginative, sensitive, sincere, cautious, adaptable, gentle, easygoing, refined, moderate, calm, optimistic, orderly, friendly, romantic, sympathetic, pleasant, honest.

## Life Challenge for Sheep

To develop confidence in their own abilities and to take more risks in life.

## The Sheep Lover

Sheep are very sexy people who are intuitively aware of their partners' and their own sexual natures. This is a fertile sign. Sheep are romantic, caring and sensitive lovers who will want to experience many lovers before settling down.

While Sheep can be a little self-conscious about their bodies and big sexual appetites, they are not so quiet as to let their needs go unfulfilled. Sheep will let you know tactfully exactly what makes them happy. Once committed, Sheep make faithful and considerate partners.

## The Sheep Family Member

The security and stability of family life suits Sheep, and can act as a source of inspiration and support to fuel their creative talents. Nostalgic to the extreme, Sheep will fill their homes with family photos and display many mementos of their families' important occasions.

Sheep make considerate and easygoing partners, and patient and nurturing parents. They are able to maintain good communication and close ties with their children. Sheep are the peacemakers in their families, and strive to keep their home environment harmonious.

## The Sheep Friend

Kindhearted and generous of spirit, Sheep make very understanding friends who will stick by their pals through thick and thin. It is the Sheep friend to whom all turn for a shoulder to cry on and a sympathetic ear. Sheep are non-judgmental, and find it easy to forgive.

While they like to socialize and are very good at bringing people together, Sheep frequently need time alone to rest and rejuvenate.

## The Sheep at Work

Sheep are much liked by their employers and colleagues, who find them friendly and very good with detail and analytical work. Sheep may be particular with their own work, and others may perceive them as perfectionists.

Sheep need a supportive, stress-free work environment in order to perform, and frequently fall ill if their workplace becomes chaotic. If they pursue their artistic talents, they need a degree of freedom to allow their imaginations to wander unhindered.

Not overly ambitious in the traditional sense, Sheep are motivated not by money or power, but by creative license and the enjoyment of harmonious relationships.

## Ideal Occupations for Sheep

Writer, poet, musician, artist, actor, therapist, religious minister, architect, gardener.

## The Five Sheep Types

### *Wood Sheep: 1955, 2015*

Wood strengthens Sheep's creative talents, so that Wood Sheep usually end up as humble artists or musicians. Wood Sheep are also very compassionate and generous people, and have a large number of friends throughout their lifetime.

### *Fire Sheep: 1967*

Fire adds some passion and energy to the normally reserved and patient Sheep. Fire Sheep are more confident in their own abilities and use their personal charm to get what they want from others.

### *Earth Sheep: 1919, 1979*

The effect of double earth on the Sheep's character is to heighten all of its inherent traits. Earth Sheep are shining examples of strong moral beliefs. Many Earth Sheep are deeply spiritual and are attracted to religion or missionary work as a career.

### *Metal Sheep: 1931, 1991*

Metal strengthens the Sheep's character. Metal Sheep display a more forthright and determined side to their personalities and have no trouble persevering through all manner of obstacles to achieve their desires.

### *Water Sheep: 1943, 2003*

Water heightens the Sheep's emotions and intuition. Water Sheep are supersensitive to everyone and everything around them, which can cause them to be highly stressed and anxious individuals. Water Sheep are advised to undertake a lot of self-development and relaxation courses.

# Relationship Chart for Sheep

*See page 16 for an explanation of the ratings used in this chart.*

| Sheep & | Rating | Potential for Harmony in Love, Friendship and Professional Life |
|---|---|---|
| **Hare** | 5 | Both have loving and caring natures, and will draw out and motivate each other. Hare will help Sheep set priorities for his or her responsibilities. Sheep will give Hare unconditional love. |
| **Pig** | 5 | Both are sensitive and understanding, and will be supportive of each other. The environment will be so tranquil that their creative talents will flourish. |
| **Rat** | 2 | Interest in each other will be only fleeting and marginally rewarding. Rat will need more than just Sheep's adoring devotion in order to maintain interest, and Sheep will feel hurt by Rat's dwindling attraction. |
| **Tiger** | 3 | Apart from their high sex drives, Tiger and Sheep will have little else in common. Sheep will be hurt by Tiger's need for adventure and personal space. Tiger will soon feel too claustrophobic. |
| **Dragon** | 2 | This pair are stark opposites, and will struggle to find anything in common or to appreciate in the other. Dragon will demand adventure, while Sheep will want stability. |
| **Snake** | 3 | There is enough mutual interest in art, music and theater for these two to be friends. However, Sheep is sentimental and sensitive, and will soon be put off by Snake's detachment. |
| **Horse** | 4 | These two will have much in common, especially creative ability, which they will encourage and help to develop in the other. The only hurdle will be Horse's lack of commitment. |
| **Sheep** | 3 | This relationship will be warm and even-tempered, as neither will want to offend the other. However, at least one of them will need to take care of the practical side of their lives if they are to survive. |
| **Monkey** | 4 | Monkey will soon have Sheep laughing at his or herself and be more willing to take risks, while Sheep will instill some morals in Monkey, and curb his or her excesses. |
| **Rooster** | 2 | Each suffers from personal insecurities, which will make this an unproductive pairing. Rooster will not be able to understand Sheep's introversion. Sheep will feel embarrassed by Rooster's flamboyance. |
| **Dog** | 4 | As both are very tolerant, these two will be able to understand and appreciate each other's differences. Dog will generally find Sheep a moral ally. Sheep will appreciate Dog's protection. |
| **Ox** | 1 | Ox will have no respect for the excitable and morally deviant sheep, who will find no excitement in the dull Ox. This pairing is best avoided, as the values and beliefs of the two will be directly opposed. |

# The Monkey

1920, 1932, 1944, 1956, 1968, 1980, 1992, 2004, 2016

**Natural Energy: Yang**
**Natural Element: Metal**

Monkey's ninth position at Buddha's side denotes mental agility. Monkeys have quick, lively intellects and sharp wits that few can match. They spend their days scheming and hatching outrageous plots and ingenious plans; they are not above manipulating others to get their own way. Monkeys like to defy convention and live strange and unusual lives.

Monkeys are also renowned tricksters and teasers, the clever and active clowns of the Chinese zodiac who search for fun and excitement in everything they do. They are irrepressible eccentrics, and highly intelligent.

## Character Traits of Monkeys

Intelligent, witty, entertaining, inquisitive, energetic, optimistic, sexual, competitive, lively, inventive, sociable, talkative, enthusiastic, generous, versatile, restless.

## Life Challenge for Monkeys

To develop self-discipline for their projects and self-control in their relationships.

## The Monkey Lover

Monkeys are charmers and naughty lovers, who like to lead promiscuous lifestyles. As they often lack morals, anything usually goes in their love lives. They often attract the unusual in sexual pleasures and the mysterious in lovers. Variety and quantity are the keys to a happy love life for Monkeys.

As Monkeys are quite competitive they will thrill to the challenge and chase of new conquests, but will run a mile at the first sign of physical struggle with other suitors.

## The Monkey Family Member

It is rare to see a domesticated Monkey, and even rarer to see a happily domesticated Monkey. Should Monkeys choose to settle down, it will only be to secure a home base from which to venture forth in search of fun and adventure.

As they hate convention and routine, they will put a lot of energy into keeping their home life exciting. Expect an open-house environment where many different people from all walks of life are invited home — indefinitely. Children will identify with the eternal child within their Monkey parent.

## The Monkey Friend

Sociable and entertaining, Monkeys demonstrate the extreme in extroversion. They hate their own company, and will therefore collect lots of friends and keep in constant contact with them. With their witty and lively conversations, Monkeys are never boring to be around.

It is rare to find someone who feels ambivalent about Monkeys. You can be sure they will keep their friends happily entertained with all their clever antics.

## The Monkey at Work

Monkeys usually win and lose fortunes repeatedly throughout their lives, as they are attracted to the riskiest of schemes.

In the workplace, Monkeys hate routine and hard work, and have short attention spans. They are not the easiest or the most pleasant to work with, but are sure to add brightness to any dull office environment. They are likely to have up-and-down careers, with a lot of erratic job changes.

At their best, Monkeys are exceptional planners and organizers who need lots of variety and challenge to keep them motivated and their highly active minds engaged.

## Ideal Occupations for Monkeys

Comedian, entertainer, actor, traveler, photographer, social columnist, journalist.

## The Five Monkey Types

### Wood Monkeys: 1944, 2004

The stability of wood dilutes some of Monkey's rather eccentric and rash traits. Wood Monkeys are more focused, less erratic and hence more capable than the average Monkey. They are the most comfortable and secure Monkeys to be around.

### Fire Monkeys: 1956, 2016

Monkey's natural metal element combines with fire to form quite powerful and ruthless individuals. Fire Monkeys are passionate and don't mind applying a little physical force as a last resort. Fire Monkeys are the most competitive and dangerous of the group.

### Earth Monkeys: 1968

The effect of the earth element is to make these Monkeys fairly interested in pursuing their intellectual development. Earth Monkeys read widely and are likely to hold numerous qualifications from an early age. They are diligent and focused.

### Metal Monkeys: 1920, 1980

The effect of double metal is to make these Monkeys quite ambitious, intelligent and very good with money. Metal Monkeys are extremely confident of their own abilities and have little trouble convincing others of their rarely matched talents.

### Water Monkeys: 1932, 1992

The water element ensures that these Monkeys are more considerate and more understanding of their effect on others, so they are less inclined to ridicule people. Water Monkeys are the team players of the group, able to cooperate and keep a check on their emotions.

# Relationship Chart for Monkeys

*See page 16 for an explanation of the ratings used in this chart.*

| Monkey & | Rating | Potential for Harmony in Love, Friendship and Professional Life |
|---|---|---|
| **Rat** | 5 | Each will admire the other's quick wit and superior intelligence. Provided Rat remains tolerant of Monkey's antics, these two will be able to initiate many schemes and ingenious plans together. |
| **Dragon** | 5 | Dragon will be attracted to Monkey's charm and wit, and Monkey to Dragon's personal power. Monkey will be happy for Dragon to dominate, and the two will live easily together. |
| **Ox** | 3 | Ox will be fascinated by Monkey's sparkling wit, and Monkey will appreciate the attention. However, the attraction will be only brief, as Monkey craves change and Ox respects routine. |
| **Hare** | 2 | Both are witty and inventive, which will ensure an attraction. However, Monkey will always be breaking social rules and norms, and Hare won't tolerate this for long. |
| **Snake** | 4 | There is enough mental dexterity to ensure their success as business partners. Snake will provide the logic, and Monkey the calculated risks. |
| **Horse** | 3 | Each will be attracted to the other's energy and enthusiasm. However, Horse wears his or her heart on his or her sleeve and can be a little gullible, which secretive Monkey will not appreciate. |
| **Sheep** | 4 | Monkey will soon have Sheep laughing at his or herself and be more willing to take risks, while Sheep will instill some morals in Monkey and curb his or her excesses. |
| **Monkey** | 3 | These two deserve each other, and will feel they have found their match in wit and intelligence. As long as they can resist feeding the rivalry between them, a relationship will develop. |
| **Rooster** | 4 | There is a lot of potential with this pairing, as both are vibrant entertainers. Rooster and Monkey need to restrain themselves from judging the other too quickly, znd to ensure they see all of the qualities the other offers. |
| **Dog** | 2 | Dog will be attracted to Monkey's intelligence, but will soon find Monkey devious and insincere. Monkey will be attracted to Dog's eagerness to please, but will find Dog's morals hard to abide. |
| **Pig** | 2 | There will be a lot of attraction between these two. However, Monkey will not be able to resist using easygoing Pig as the butt of his or her jokes. Pigs will soon be left feeling hurt and dejected. |
| **Tiger** | 1 | Both are competitive and impatient daredevils, ensuring many calamities. Tiger will be supersensitive to Monkey's pranks, and Monkey will soon get bored with Tiger's lack of appreciation. |

# The Rooster

1921, 1933, 1945, 1957, 1969, 1981, 1993, 2005, 2017

*Natural Energy: Yin*
*Natural Element: Metal*

Rooster's tenth position at Buddha's side denotes strength, alertness and honor — usually military honor. Roosters are flamboyant people who are attracted to pomp and ceremony in social occasions. Appearances mean everything to Roosters, who spend much time on their looks and like to be admired more for their appearance than their intelligence.

Roosters can be sensitive to and easily influenced by others' flattery, criticism or ridicule, and are likely to be critical of others in turn. Roosters are gutsy people who demonstrate a lot of bluff and bravado, and like to speak their minds. They are not necessarily tactful or cautious. Many Roosters are avid readers — although they generally keep this a secret, as they want to be admired for their presence rather than their questioning minds.

## Character Traits of Roosters

Flamboyant, resourceful, courageous, resilient, cultivated, capable, entertaining, critical, proud, knowledgable, ambitious, frank, extravagant, protective, impulsive, provocative.

## Life Challenge for Roosters

To believe truly in themselves and rely less on others' opinions.

## The Rooster Lover

As a lover, Rooster needs to be the boss — they must be in control of all of their relationships. Every love affair will be conducted on their terms, and should their partners oblige, Roosters will generously reward them with expensive dinners, fine wine, exotic holidays and lavish presents.

As appearances mean everything, Roosters will put a lot of energy into their sexual performance and may be critical of their partners. To win their hearts and soften their exterior armor, the frequent use of flattery and lavish praise is essential.

## The Rooster Family Member

Roosters have high expectations of their partners and children, and want them to shine in any social gathering. Hence Roosters can be demanding and not the easiest to live with. However, they are generous to the extreme and will protect their families and homes to the death if need be. The Rooster child displays these same traits, and is also a keen reader who shows scholastic potential.

Roosters can make a vibrant addition to any family, provided they have a special place in their home to relax and collect their wits. Family members need to learn not to be offended by the Rooster's occasional blasts of hot wind.

## The Rooster Friend

Roosters love to entertain — they will go all out with dress, catering and furnishings to impress their guests. Addicted to compliments, Roosters will put much energy into decorating their homes with the latest style, and may be obsessed with cleanliness.

As Roosters like to be held in high esteem by their friends, they are generous with their time and possessions. In their much-needed quiet time, Roosters will indulge their private passion of reading.

## The Rooster at Work

Roosters' love for ceremony and tradition will see them attracted to professional careers in the military or the police force. In fact, any profession that requires a uniform will appear impressive and dramatic to the Rooster.

Roosters work hard, and attend to details, for the accolades that a job well done will bring them, thought they will not necessarily receive much pleasure from the work itself. Articulate and knowledgable, Roosters know how to gain attention, and will not go unnoticed in any work environment. Therefore, professions that provide them with a lot of attention will suit them.

## Ideal Occupations for Roosters

TV show host, military officer, public relations officer, sales person, critic, academic, actor, model, police officer.

## The Five Rooster Types

### *Wood Roosters: 1945, 2005*

The wood element provides Roosters with the opportunity to gain wisdom throughout their lives. Wood Roosters are less hot tempered and more easy going than the average Rooster, and will prefer spending their time in quiet pursuit of knowledge.

### *Fire Roosters: 1957, 2017*

Fire adds more heat to Roosters' already passionate and daring personalities. Fire Roosters are bold people in both their dress and manner. They have presence and, as they are not swayed too much by others' opinions, can attain high public positions.

### *Earth Roosters: 1969*

The earth element ensures that these Roosters are more grounded and resourceful than the other types. Earth Roosters are not as flamboyant or argumentative. As they are more self-controlled, they have more ability to manage their personal finances.

### *Metal Roosters: 1921, 1981*

The effect of double metal is to make these Roosters even more resolute and uncompromising in manner. Metal Roosters are perfectionists who set high standards for themselves and others. Supercritical of everything and everyone, they may be difficult to get along with.

### *Water Roosters: 1933, 1993*

Water provides these Roosters with more personal adaptability and more empathy for others. Water Roosters enjoy their social activities and are attractive to a wider audience. Less self-obsessed than the other Roosters, the delightful Water Roosters are a pleasure to have around.

# Relationship Chart for Roosters

*See page 16 for an explanation of the ratings used in this chart.*

| Rooster & | Rating | Potential for Harmony in Love, Friendship and Professional Life |
|---|---|---|
| Ox | 5 | Much success could come from this pairing, as flamboyant Rooster will attend to the social aspects of the relationship, while Ox will attend to the detailed planning and physical work. |
| Snake | 5 | Each will complement and have respect for the other. Snake will admire Rooster's flamboyant social presence. Rooster will appreciate Snake's wise counsel and social refinement. |
| Rat | 2 | Each will be too quick to misjudge the other. Rat will view Rooster as too flamboyant and superficial, while Rooster will lose patience with Rat's cool and controlled exterior. |
| Tiger | 3 | Each will be attracted to the other's appearance, but Rooster and Tiger will have very different communication styles. Rooster will henpeck Tiger on every detail, which will frustrate carefree Tiger no end. |
| Dragon | 3 | Mutual attraction is assured, as Dragon and Rooster regularly share the limelight. Unfortunately, neither will be too interested in a committed relationship with the other. |
| Horse | 3 | Both are lively and entertaining, which ensures initial attraction. However, Rooster will want to control the relationship, which will cause Horse to bolt. |
| Sheep | 2 | Each suffers from personal insecurities, which will make this an unproductive pairing. Rooster will not be able to understand Sheep's introversion. Sheep will feel embarrassed by Rooster's flamboyance. |
| Monkey | 4 | There is a lot of potential with this pairing, as both are lively entertainers. Both need to restrain his or herself from judging the other too quickly, to ensure he or she see all of the qualities the other offers. |
| Rooster | 3 | An exotic and attractive pairing, they will maintain an extensive social life. As each will fight for control, they will need to exercise restraint and understanding. |
| Dog | 2 | Each has different values and beliefs. Dog will find Rooster egotistical and self-absorbed. Rooster will find Dog too moralistic and unselfish for his or her own good. |
| Pig | 4 | Pig will be happy for Rooster to rule, and will be understanding of Rooster's secret insecurities. Rooster will appreciate Pig's support, and will reward Pig with generosity. |
| Hare | 1 | Rooster and Hare are poles apart in their values and social styles, and hence little respect will be achieved. Hare is considerate and understated, and Rooster fairly self-absorbed. |

# The Dog

1922, 1934, 1946, 1958, 1970, 1982, 1994, 2006, 2018

*Natural Energy: Yang*
*Natural Element: Earth*

Dog's 11th position at Buddha's side stands for loyalty and justice. People born in Dog years are idealistic and highly principled. They have strong beliefs and live by their morals. To a Dog everything in life is either black or white, right or wrong, good or bad: there is no middle ground. Dogs hate injustice, insincerity and disloyalty.

Dogs are champions of the downtrodden, loyal supporters of just causes, and totally self-sacrificing. They need a purpose in life in order to feel content, and will often put the interests of others before their own. Alert, watchful and perceptive, Dogs are cautious and rely on their instincts to pick just the right time to jump and make their mark.

## Character Traits of Dogs

Loyal, dutiful, unselfish, honest, idealistic, courageous, trustworthy, tolerant, faithful, responsible, anxious, capable, honorable, kind, generous, compassionate, heroic.

## Life Challenge for Dogs

To love and care for themselves and to learn to ask for what they want.

## The Dog Lover

Dogs make thoughtful and loyal lovers who take their time falling in love. Dog lovers are more affectionate than passionate, and can easily become hurt and depressed by the words and actions of their lovers. Once Dogs commit they become deeply attached to their partners and can be a little possessive.

Dogs' partners will need to reward their faithful Dog lovers with lots of praise and reassurance to relieve them of their general anxiety about the relationship and their jealousy and suspicions.

## The Dog Family Member

Children can identify with Dog's basic nature — friendly, straightforward, playful — and hence adore their Dog parent. Likewise, Dog parents adore their children. Good communication and strong relationships exist in Dog households, as Dogs are patient and good listeners.

Dogs also make good providers for their families and are not above sacrificing their own dreams and desires to provide for their partners and children. In China it is the Dogs who are the ultimate family protectors, and any family lucky enough to contain a Dog parent will be blessed with much security and comfort.

## The Dog Friend

Dogs appear a little reserved, even aloof, in large gatherings, and do not make friends instantly. They prefer to play keen observer for a while in order to assess a person's nature before approaching him or her for friendly conversation.

Once Dogs make friends, they are loyal and trusting for life. While generous with their own time and possessions, they will not ask for much in return, and are quite understanding about and forgiving of any faults in their friends.

## The Dog at Work

More than anything, Dogs need to be proud of their professions and so seek meaningful work. They are usually involved in humanitarian causes or in improving social justice. They like responsibility and clear direction, preferably in a team environment. Dogs are not materialistic and are motivated more by their personal sense of achievement than they are by money. Dogs are not good left on their own.

Dogs are respected and much confided in by their employers and colleagues, because of their tireless hard work, competent decision making and devotion to the firm. These traits alone will see many Dogs quickly and effortlessly reach high positions.

## Ideal Occupations for Dogs

Charity worker, missionary, lawyer, judge, doctor, police officer, religious leader.

## The Five Dog Types

*Wood Dogs: 1934, 1994*

The wood element makes these Dogs more open to new experiences and less judgmental. Wood Dogs can see and understand the "gray" in situations and are therefore the most empathetic of all the Dog family.

*Fire Dogs : 1946, 2006*

Fire builds passion and confidence in Dogs. Fire Dogs can balance the needs of others with their own and, as such, are less humble and more confident than most Dogs. They are charismatic, and can win support easily.

*Earth Dogs: 1958, 2018*

Double earth helps to balance Dogs' anxieties and phobias. Earth Dogs are quite stable and reliable and less prone to stress. Earth Dogs are realistic, and very practical. They are good with methodical and detailed work.

*Metal Dogs: 1970*

Metal strengthens Dogs' ideals and moral beliefs. Metal Dogs are forthright and like to speak their minds. They may lead chaste lives, and will often be attracted to self-sacrificing work in charities or religion — far more so than any other type of Dog.

*Water Dogs: 1922, 1982*

Water makes these Dogs more adaptable and intuitive. Water Dogs are big "softies" emotionally and are prone to taking in and caring for all the local strays. They fill their homes with unconditional love and acceptance. They are pure angels and invaluable to society.

## Relationship Chart for Dogs

*See page 16 for an explanation of the ratings used in this chart.*

| Dog & | Rating | Potential for Harmony in Love, Friendship and Professional Life |
|---|---|---|
| **Tiger** | 5 | There will be much understanding and respect between these two. The practical Dog will ease Tiger's impulsiveness, and energetic Tiger will chase away Dog's anxieties and inner doubts. |
| **Horse** | 5 | A solid relationship of similar temperaments and respect. Dog will understand Horse's need for freedom and will be supportive. Horse will openly demonstrate appreciation, which Dog will cherish. |
| **Rat** | 3 | This pairing can work if kept at friendship level. Both signs are nagged by personal insecurities, which can accumulate with this pairing. Rat's secrecy will be misinterpreted by Dog as underhanded scheming. |
| **Ox** | 4 | Dogs and Oxen share common values such as loyalty and respect. This pairing could work if Ox can lighten up and if Dog can maintain an understanding of Ox's temperament. |
| **Hare** | 3 | The two have similar temperaments and are likely to put each other's needs before their own. While there will be little conflict, there will also be not much challenge between them or much initiative taken. |
| **Snake** | 2 | In the long run, this combination will work only with difficulty. Snake tends to be intense and secretive, and the honorable and upfront Dog is likely to see this as deceit. |
| **Sheep** | 4 | As both are very tolerant, Dog and Sheep will understand and appreciate each other's differences. Dog will generally find Sheep a moral ally. Sheep will appreciate Dog's protection. |
| **Monkey** | 2 | Dog will be attracted to Monkey's intelligence, but will soon find Monkey devious and insincere. Monkey will be attracted to Dog's eagerness to please, but will find Dog's morals hard to abide. |
| **Rooster** | 2 | Each has different values and beliefs. Dog will find Rooster egotistical and self-absorbed. Rooster will find Dog too moralistic and unselfish for his or her own good. |
| **Dog** | 3 | Compassionate and caring, two Dogs could have a wonderfully fulfilling relationship, provided they throw caution to the wind on occasion and engage in some risk taking. |
| **Pig** | 4 | Pig will be able to uplift Dog from his or her worries, and Dog will find his or herself cherished as faithful protectors. There will be much opportunity for success, if both can avoid excessive moralizing. |
| **Dragon** | 1 | There will be little attraction between these two. Their moral beliefs will vary in the extreme. Egotistical Dragon will make Dog snap often, and exhausting fights will result. |

# The Pig

1923, 1935, 1947, 1959, 1971, 1983, 1995, 2007, 2019

***Natural Energy: Yin***
***Natural Element: Water***

The 12th and final position at Buddha's side represents completion and celebration of the cycle's end. Pigs are the most easily contented and happy-go-lucky of all the Chinese zodiac animals. They are true peacemakers and talented at bringing divergent groups and individuals together in harmony.

Carefree and good-natured, Pigs don't demand much from others, are easy to get along with, and like to live in peaceful and secure surrounds. Happy and sociable, they prefer to spend most of their time indulging in social gaiety and enjoying gourmet cuisine.

### Character Traits of Pigs

Sensual, eager, caring, indulgent, pleasure seeking, fun, lighthearted, optimistic, warmhearted, peaceful, flexible, understanding, generous, happy, shy, modest, sentimental.

### Life Challenge for Pigs

To set specific goals in their lives and to apply sufficient energy to ensure their goals are accomplished.

### The Pig Lover

Pigs are quite happy to wallow in sensuous love making for long stretches of time, and will demonstrate a lot of tender loving care and deep emotions toward their lovers. As Pigs are also considerate and understanding, they are able to forgive their partners' many trespasses before finally letting go.

In return, Pigs seek good providers and protectors in their lovers, who will often be happy to provide Pigs with the means to pursue their sensual indulgences and pleasures.

## The Pig Family Member

"Home Sweet Home" is where most Pigs really want to be. Pigs are in their element when surrounded by a close and caring family. They are true nurturers, and prefer to stay at home while their partners go off to work to earn the family's bacon.

The Chinese believe a Pig brings much happiness to a family, and hence Pig children are always a delight. As parents, Pigs will want their own children to be achievers, so can be a little strict with them to ensure they grow up disciplined — a trait they lack themselves.

## The Pig Friend

As the most affable, easygoing and undemanding animals of the zodiac, Pigs are assured of many friendships. Their sincerity, genuineness and overall concern for others' well-being all ensure they are often sought out for their advice, support and warm company.

As a busy social life and indulging in fine food are important to them, Pigs will put much energy into social arrangements. Friends of Pigs can look forward to many picnics, dinner parties and social gatherings, where fine food will always be present.

## The Pig at Work

If they didn't have to work, Pigs wouldn't. To most Pigs, work is but a means to an end. They rarely put energy into planning their careers, preferring them to unravel unhindered while they keep focused on their families and enjoy their friendships.

However, Pigs are liked and appreciated by everyone at work and make enthusiastic team members. Always eager to please, and particularly where their own work is concerned, Pigs take their individual responsibilities quite seriously. Many Pigs end up pursuing successful careers as independent artists or craftspeople.

## Ideal Occupations for Pigs

Homemaker, childcare worker, nurse, counselor, chef, artist, diplomat, government worker.

## The Five Pig Types

### *Wood Pigs: 1935, 1995*

The wood element provides an emphasis on Pig's communication skills. Wood Pigs are good at communicating their thoughts and feelings, and are able to express their needs. Wood Pigs are encouraged to consider careers as counselors or diplomats, where they can use these skills to the fullest.

### *Fire Pigs: 1947, 2007*

The fire element gets these Pigs moving and adds some bravado and risk taking to their home-loving characters. Fire Pigs are more ambitious and more likely to seek careers that ensure some travel and moderate adventure. Fire can also heighten Pigs' eagerness, which could lead them into situations they cannot handle.

### *Earth Pigs: 1959, 2019*

Earth Pigs are the true homebodies of the Pig family. The big wide world holds little interest for Earth Pigs, who are quite happy to settle down early in life and lead a routine and secure existence. It's the simple, everyday pleasures that attract Earth Pigs.

### *Metal Pigs: 1971*

Metal provides Pigs with much-needed strength of character and tenacity. Metal Pigs are ambitious, while also fairly sociable. They blend together the various areas of their life well. Metal Pigs have a tendency to be extra stubborn.

### *Water Pigs: 1923, 1983*

The double water element heightens Pigs' heavy emotional and intuitive state, making Water Pigs supersensitive and emotionally indulgent. Lost in a world of personal introspection and prone to depression, Water Pigs may lack the physical and mental fortitude required for picking themselves up out of a rut.

# Relationship Chart for Pigs

*See page 16 for an explanation of the ratings used in this chart.*

| Pig & | Rating | Potential for Harmony in Love, Friendship and Professional Life |
|---|---|---|
| **Hare** | 5 | Both have peaceful and tolerant natures, and will be able to provide each other with gentle, loving care. Pig will provide strength and openness, and Hare practicality. |
| **Sheep** | 5 | Both are sensitive and understanding, and will be supportive of each other. The environment will be so tranquil that their creative talents will flourish. |
| **Rat** | 3 | The sensuous Pig will revel in Rat's material acquisitions. Rat will enjoy the provider role at first, and will then be likely to take the Pig for granted, leaving little hope for long-term success. |
| **Ox** | 3 | Both crave a peaceful and quiet home life. However, Pig may be irresponsible with money, which will frustrate Ox. Unless Pig can learn restraint, Ox will soon leave. |
| **Tiger** | 4 | Home-loving Pig will be happy and appreciative if Tiger acts as provider and protector. Tiger will bask in Pig's esteem and indulgent nature. |
| **Dragon** | 4 | This pairing is an example of opposites attracting. Dramatic Dragon will sweep easygoing Pig off his or her feet. Pig will reward Dragon with adoration and esteem. |
| **Horse** | 4 | This couple will be popular and will have an active social life together. At some point Horse will want to travel abroad and Pig will want to stay at home. |
| **Monkey** | 2 | There will be a lot of attraction between these two. However, Monkey will not be able to resist using easygoing Pig as butt of his or her jokes. Pig will soon be left feeling hurt and dejected. |
| **Rooster** | 2 | Pig will be happy for Rooster to rule, and will be understanding of his or her secret insecurities. Rooster will appreciate Pig's support, and will reward his or her with generosity. |
| **Dog** | 4 | Pig will be able to uplift Dog from his or her worries, and Dog will find his or herself cherished as faithful protectors. There is opportunity for success, if both can avoid moralizing. |
| **Pig** | 3 | Two Pigs together will be very happy, but will have little self-control. Each will encourage the other to overindulge in life's pleasures, with little regard for practicalities or consequences. |
| **Snake** | 1 | Pig is open and generous with affection. Snake is secretive, and keeps feelings to him or herself. The two just will not be able understand or respect each other. |

# Famous Profiles

## Famous Rats

### Water Rat: George Washington, first US President (1732)

George Washington gained recognition as the first US President. He demonstrated great oratory skills and had wide public appeal — specific traits associated with Water Rats.

### Fire Rat: Mata Hari, spy (1876)

Mata Hari was a world-famous spy for Germany during World War I. A skilled seductress, she displayed the wit and charm for which Fire Rats are famous. She was able to obtain highly confidential military secrets from her intimate relationships with high-ranking Allied officers.

## Famous Oxen

### Wood Ox: Paul Newman, Actor & philanthropist (1925)

Paul Newman is a Wood Ox who exhibits this Ox's intense goal orientation and ethical approach to life. Devoted to his family, Newman has at the same time maintained a highly successful acting and business career.

### Metal Ox: Diana, Princess of Wales (1961)

Princess Diana was a Metal Ox who clearly demonstrated this Ox type's tenacity and ambition with her transformation from retiring kindergarten aide to the sophisticated Princess of Wales. She was a typical traditionalist Ox, persevering through all manner of hardship to fulfill her goals and obligations.

## Famous Tigers

### Fire Tiger: Hugh Hefner, publisher (1926)

Hugh Hefner is a Fire Tiger who displays this Tiger's double dose of passion and energy. Creating the Playboy empire from humble beginnings, Hefner has attracted much publicity and notoriety as a fast-living businessman, and has enjoyed many a love affair, for which Tigers are famous.

### Water Tiger: Jody Foster, actor (1962)

Jody Foster is a calmer Tiger who has achieved the rare feat of successfully moving from child actor to a highly acclaimed adult actor. Water Tigers are intuitive and are gifted communicators. An acting career is an ideal choice of profession for these Tigers.

## Famous Hares

### Water Hare: Cary Grant, actor (1904)

Cary Grant holds the title of the most debonair and stylish of all the matinee idols. His polished style, eloquence and flawless manners are characteristic of the Water Hare and made him the most coveted romantic leading man during the 1930s, 1940s and 1950s.

### Wood Hare: Ingrid Bergman, actor (1915)

Ingrid Bergman has exhibited the Hare's trademark cool exterior and refinement as an actor. Wood Hares are noted for their artistic talents, and Ingrid Bergman certainly displayed hers as a gifted actress of both stage and screen in Europe and the USA.

## Famous Dragons

### Fire Dragon: Harold Robbins, author (1916)

Harold Robbins is famous for his gripping novels involving drama and intrigue. Fire Dragons have double the passion and vibrancy of other Dragons, which Robbins is obviously able to channel into his exciting epics.

### Earth Dragon: Eartha Kitt, singer (1928)

Eartha Kitt is a more balanced Dragon who displays the classic individualistic traits for which Dragons are famous. With her distinctive voice and stage presence, Eartha won much acclaim in her role as the Cat Woman in the early Batman and Robin series.

## Famous Snakes

### Earth Snake: Mahatma Gandhi, political/social leader (1869)

Gandhi displayed all the shrewdness, intuitiveness and political savvy for which Snakes are famous. He was also a calm and caring person, a particular trait of Earth Snakes. Gandhi certainly used all the traits of his animal and element sign in his chosen profession.

### Earth Snake: Jackie Kennedy Onassis, US First Lady (1929)

Jackie Kennedy Onassis followed her Snake's natural instinct to marry well. She won much praise and respect as a stylish and politically savvy US First Lady, wife of John F. Kennedy. She later married for a time the Greek billionaire Aristotle Onassis, and maintained her reputation for cultured elegance till her death.

## Famous Horses

### Metal Horse: Sean Connery, actor (1930)

Sean Connery displays all the youthful vitality and dexterity for which Horses are famous, and also the typical headstrong and resolute traits that are specific to Metal Horses. A versatile actor who, like all Horses, has aged gracefully, Connery has appealed to all in his heroic, action-packed movie roles.

### Water Horse: Barbra Streisand, actor/singer (1942)

Streisand displays all the communicative and artistic ability renowned in Water Horses, with her versatile skills as an actor, singer, producer and director. A typical Horse, She has also aged well and is known to be a perfectionist in her performances.

## Famous Sheep

### Water Sheep: John Denver, singer/songwriter (1943)

Denver displayed the Sheep's typical creative and peaceful mind with his songs of love and nature. Also an environmentalist, John Denver was able to relieve his stress and achieve emotional balance by spending much of his time in the US Rocky Mountains.

### Earth Sheep: Margot Fonteyn, ballerina (1919)

Fonteyn followed her artistic calling, present in many Sheep, and achieved worldwide acclaim as a ballerina. The presence of the double earth element ensured she was able to stay focused on her dance technique, and to adapt herself easily to any dance role.

## Famous Monkeys

### Fire Monkey: Mel Gibson, actor (1956)

Gibson, a Fire Monkey, embodies the fun-loving larrikin in all Monkeys. He is renowned on movie sets for playing endless pranks and tricks on his co-stars. As a Fire Monkey, Mel Gibson is also quite competitive, and enjoys physical challenges, which is evident in many of his movie roles.

### Earth Monkey: Bette Davis, actor (1908)

Bette Davis is a legend among film stars. As a typical Earth Monkey, she exhibited a more serious side to her personality, and her mental agility was evident in the roles she played on screen. Like many Monkeys, she had a strong effect: the public either loved her or loathed her.

# Famous Roosters

### Metal Rooster: Peter Ustinov, actor/producer/writer (1921)

Ustinov is a fine example of Roosters' love of pomp and ceremony. As a Metal Rooster, he can be headstrong, and particular in his work. His acting and writing have displayed his vibrant disposition.

### Water Rooster: Joan Collins, actor (1933)

A typical Water Rooster, Joan Collins loves social activities, portraying the role of rich, immaculate social queen with perfection. Dripping in diamonds and clothed in nothing but high fashion, she automatically lights up every socially significant occasion, clearly displaying the Water Rooster traits.

# Famous Dogs

### Wood Dog: Elvis Presley, singer (1935)

Presley honored his mother and remained close to his father throughout his life, which is classic behavior for all Dogs. As a Wood Dog Elvis was empathetic toward others, and deplored spending time alone. His Gracelands mansion was more often than not an open house to all his family, friends and colleagues.

### Wood Dog: Shirley MacLaine, actor/writer (1934)

MacLaine is a classic example of a Dog in pursuit of the truth. In her books, Shirley MacLaine explains her search for and experience of a higher consciousness and describes her theories on the meaning of life.

# Famous Pigs

### Wood Pig: Dudley Moore, comedian/actor/musician (1935)

Moore is the model happy-go-lucky, pleasure-seeking Pig, with the Wood element elevating his artistic traits. Like many Pigs, he can be easily swayed and won over by less scrupulous types. His personal life has been marked by a number of divorces.

### Metal Pig: Lucille Ball, comedian/actor (1911)

Ball indulged her humorous Pig personality and chose acting as her career. As a Metal Pig, Lucille Ball displayed more perseverance and tenacity than other Pigs, which was also evident in the roles she played: she was able to avoid falling prey to others' schemes.

# Chinese Astrology and the Western Zodiac

Why not investigate the traits of both your Chinese and Western signs, and their associated elements? This could give you a more detailed individual character profile. Also, a combined profile could identify the unique subtleties that may help determine with more accuracy your communication style and, therefore your relationship and career success.

While Chinese and Western astrology systems differ, there are some key similarities:

★ Each system has 12 core signs, often represented by an animal.
★ Each system divides the 12 signs into four groups of three,
  to highlight compatibility.
★ Each system relies on elements (earth, fire, water, air, wood, metal) to reveal
  the differences between members of each animal sign as well as commonalities
  between signs.

Here are some of the fundamental differences:

## The Chinese System

This is based on a 60-year "life cycle", within which the 12 animal signs, along with one of the five elements, rules for one whole lunar year:
12 signs x 5 elements = 60.

Each animal sign has both a primary and a dominant element influencing its traits.

## *The Western Zodiac*

This zodiac does not have a life cycle; the system is a continuum. It is based on the solar year, where each sign rules for approximately 30 days of the 365-day year. Each sign is associated with only one primary element, of which there are four.

### *Elements of the Western Zodiac*

| ELEMENT | CHARACTERISTICS |
|---------|-----------------|
| **Fire** | Passionate, energetic, courageous, wild, vibrant, unpredictable |
| **Air** | Intelligent, wise, thoughtful, analytical, cautious, detached |
| **Earth** | Grounded, practical, balanced, realistic, materialistic |
| **Water** | Emotional, intuitive, considerate, generous, flexible |

### *Signs of the Western Zodiac*

| SIGN | DATES | ELEMENT | ENERGY |
|------|-------|---------|--------|
| Aries: The Ram | 21 March–19 April | Fire | Masculine/positive |
| Taurus: The Bull | 20 April–20 May | Earth | Feminine/negative |
| Gemini: The Twins | 21 May–20 June | Air | Masculine/positive |
| Cancer: The Crab | 21 June–22 July | Water | Feminine/negative |
| Leo: The Lion | 23 July–22 August | Fire | Masculine/positive |
| Virgo: The Virgin | 23 August–22 September | Earth | Feminine/negative |
| Libra: The Scales | 23 September–22 October | Air | Masculine/positive |
| Scorpio: The Scorpion | 23 October–21 November | Water | Feminine/negative |
| Sagittarius: The Archer | 22 November–21 December | Fire | Masculine/positive |
| Capricorn: The Goat | 22 December–19 January | Earth | Feminine/negative |
| Aquarius: The Water Carrier | 20 January–18 February | Air | Masculine/positive |
| Pisces: The Fish | 19 February–20 March | Water | Feminine/negative |

## Compatibility Groups

Signs that share the same element are said to be similar. This makes them sympathethic to each other, and therefore make the best pairings for love, friendship and business. This is also true of the Chinese system.

Fire signs:    Aries, Leo, Sagittarius
Air signs:     Gemini, Libra, Aquarius
Earth signs:   Taurus, Virgo, Capricorn
Water signs:   Cancer, Scorpio, Pisces

### Character Traits for Western Zodiac Signs

| SIGN | CHARACTER TRAITS |
| --- | --- |
| Aries | Competitive, energetic, enthusiastic, impulsive, daring |
| Taurus | Patient, logical, tenacious, determined, sensuous |
| Gemini | Intelligent, articulate, witty, ingenious, perceptive |
| Cancer | Affectionate, considerate, cautious, emotional, imaginative |
| Leo | Loyal, powerful, noble, dynamic, charismatic, brave |
| Virgo | Refined, practical, proper, gentle, particular, gracious |
| Libra | Balanced, charming, intelligent, idealistic, fair |
| Scorpio | Reserved, mysterious, sensitive, alluring, calculating |
| Sagittarius | Free-spirited, open, friendly, physical, adventurous |
| Capricorn | Ambitious, hard-working, dependable, tenacious |
| Aquarius | Idealistic, innovative, individual, visionary, spiritual |
| Pisces | Creative, sensitive, emotional, intuitive, flexible |

## How To Combine the Two Systems

1. Add your Western sign traits and the associated element characteristics to those of your dominant Chinese animal sign.
2. Note the energy type of both your Chinese animal (yin or yang) and Western sign (masculine or feminine).

3. Look for similarities and contrasts among all the traits. Are specific traits heightened as a result, or are they more varied?

4. Determine if a balance is achieved between the two types of energies.

| Chinese | Western |
|---------|---------|
| Yang = | Masculine/positive |
| Yin = | Feminine/negative |

5. Do the elements vary or does one dominate? How do the characteristics of the elements influence your animal traits?

As the Chinese say, the purpose of astrology is to achieve balance and harmony through knowing better both your character and the characters of others.

## *Example 1*

**Oprah Winfrey, US talk show host – born 29 January 1954**

| | SIGN | ELEMENTS | ENERGY |
|---|------|----------|--------|
| **Chinese Profile:** | Snake | Natural: Fire<br>Dominant: Water | Yin |
| **Western Profile:** | Aquarius | Air | Masculine/positive |

## Summary of Combined Profiles

The energy is ideally balanced in Oprah's combined profile and a display of traits with a balance of elements. There is an emphasis on intellectual and intuitive ability coming from the traits of both signs.

Aquarian Snakes are ruled by their minds and make for deep and original thinkers who are skilled at sensing the mood in any situation and are able to respond appropriately. Both Snakes and Aquarians are great observers and like to take an unbiased and objective approach to life.

## Example 2

**Karen – born 11 September 1959**

|  | SIGN | ELEMENTS | ENERGY |
|---|---|---|---|
| **Chinese Profile:** | Pig | Natural: Water<br>Dominant: Earth | Yin |
| **Western Profile:** | Virgo | Earth | Feminine/Negative |

## Summary of Combined Profiles

This combination of traits shows a peaceful, almost righteous character. The emphasis of the Earth element accentuates the practical side of the personality and the combined yin energy will also have a strong effect.

Virgo pigs are very honest and considerate do-gooders, often taking on the problems of others to their own detriment. They have a clear sense of right from wrong and are not above sharing this with others. Their life's priority is to create a safe and secure home for themselves and their families, and they will sacrifice their love of self-indulgence to achieve this.

## Example 3

**Jeanette – born 25 July 1962**

|  | SIGN | ELEMENTS | ENERGY |
|---|---|---|---|
| **Chinese Profile:** | Tiger | Natural: Wood<br>Dominant: Water | Yang |
| **Western Profile:** | Leo | Fire | Masculine/Positive |

## Summary of Combined Profiles

Leo Tigers are passionate to the extreme and have dynamic personalities. The effect of Water will be to soften the Yang orientation, adding a degree of flexibility, intuition and communicative skills to these otherwise fairly powerful and energetic individuals.

# Chinese Astrology and Feng Shui

Feng shui (pronounced "foong swee" (Cantonese) or "fong shwee" (Mandarin)) is an ancient Chinese system of design and placement, based on the idea that people can be affected either positively or negatively by their surroundings.

Feng shui specialists aim to maximize the energy flow throughout every space in a person's environment. They do this by carefully considering such things as the direction, shape and color of houses, gardens, rooms, doors, windows, furniture and furnishings, and suggesting useful changes or additions.

Knowledge of your dominant animal sign (yin/yang and primary element) and associated year element will assist feng shui specialists in tailoring their recommendations to your individual needs.

## Balancing Yin and Yang Energy

*Yang animals* — rat, tiger, dragon, monkey, horse, dog — are the more naturally extroverted and physically active animals. They require specific yin-oriented features in their environment to promote rest, reflection and rejuvenation.

## Sample Yin Features for Yang Animals

Dark, wet, soft, cold, down, north, inward, receptive, curvy, round. Ways to achieve more yin are:

★ cool, dark rooms
★ rounded, curved furniture
★ soothing and relaxing music

*Yin animals* — ox, hare, snake, sheep, rooster, pig — are the more naturally introverted and physically passive animals. They require specific yang-oriented features in their environment to build their energy reserves and promote more activity.

## *Sample Yang Features for Yin Animals*

Light, dry, hard, warm or hot, up, south, outward, creative, straight, angular. Ways to achieve more yang are:
• light, bright rooms
• angular furniture
• upbeat, passionate music

## *Providing Harmony Through the Elements*

Note your animal's primary element and  the dominant element based on your year of birth in the Chinese Year Chart on pages 12–15.

The following table details some specific features identified with each element. By applying the features of your primary and dominant element/s to your environment, you can promote those characteristics in your personality. If you feel lacking in the characteristics of those elements, add the features to your environment.

| FEATURE | WOOD | FIRE | EARTH | METAL | WATER |
|---|---|---|---|---|---|
| **Direction** | East | South | Midpoint | West | North |
| **Color** | Green | Red | Yellow | White/Silver | Black/Blue |
| **Season** | Spring | Summer | All | Autumn | Winter |
| **Shape** | Tall/Column | Pointed/Triangular | Flat/low | Round | Undulating/irregular |
| **Energy** | Outward | Upward | Horizontal | Inward | Downward |

For example, in Example 2 on page 76, Karen's elements are Water and Earth: Water is the natural element to Pigs, and Earth is the element of 1959. She could add yellow and blue furnishings to her home and focus on flat and flowing features.

Remember that the elements flow in cycles, which can be either productive or destructive. So, apart from focusing only on the features of your own element, you may like to add some features of those that are missing. For example, if Karen feels that she's not moving ahead in life she may need to work on her productive cycle. As water and earth should occur naturally in her character, she could add wood and fire to her environment to get herself out of the rut she's in.

## The Productive Cycle
*Wood* ☞ *Fire* ☞ *Earth* ☞ *Metal* ☞ *Water*

In contrast, those who have a double element, i.e. where the natural and dominant elements are the same, need to reduce this build-up by applying the features of the element that can destroy it instead. For example, a person who has the same element given their animal and year of birth may be feeling stagnant. What needs to happen is the element needs to be destroyed or diluted by incorporating aspects of the element that destroys the double element. This is done by making use of the destructive cycle.

## The Destructive Cycle
*Wood* ☞ *Earth* ☞ *Water* ☞ *Fire* ☞ *Metal*

For example, water will destroy fire. People with double fire as their sole element can apply additional water features in their environments to help reduce the effect of the fire characteristics in their personalities. Features could include paintings depicting water scenes, lots of blue throughout the house or a fountain in the garden.

*The destructive cycle*

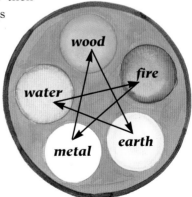

*For my colorful Water Rooster parents Trevor and Norma Burns.*
*Thank you for your unconditional love, support,*
*and encouragement to follow my dreams.*

Published by Lansdowne Publishing Pty Ltd
CEO Steven Morris: steven@lanspub.com.au

© Copyright 1998 Lansdowne Publishing Pty Ltd

First published 1999
Reprinted 2000, 2001, 2003, 2006

Commissioned by Deborah Nixon
Production Manager: Sally Stokes
Designer: Sylvie Abecassis
Editor: Avril Janks
Illustrators: Sue Ninham, Joanna Davies
Calligrapher: Joy Marden
Project Co-ordinator: Jenny Coren

National Library of Australian Cataloguing-in-Publication Data

Burns, Debbie, 1962–
Chinese horoscopes: an easy guide to the Chinese system of astrology.

Bibliography.
Includes index.
ISBN 1 86302 651 7

1. Astrology, Chinese I. Title

133.59251

All rights reserved. No part of this publication may be reproduced, stored
in a retrieval system, or transmitted in any form, or by any means, electronic,
mechanical, photocopying, recording, or otherwise, without the prior written
permission of the publisher.

Set in Cochin on QuarkXPress
Printed in Singapore by Tien Wah Press (Pte) Ltd